I SHALL BE CLEAN

By
Linda Mather

I shall be clean

Copyright © [2012] by [Linda Mather]
All rights reserved.

ISBN- 13: 978-1480020856
ISBN- 10: 1480020850

Cover art by dreamstime

This book contains material under International and Federal Copyright Laws and Treaties. Any unauthorised reprint or use of this material is prohibited. No part of this book may be reproduced or transmitted in any form or by any means, electronic or mechanical, including photocopying, recording or by any information storage or retrieval system without express written permission from the author.

I shall be clean

Author

Linda was born in Easington Colliery, Co Durham in 1958, and then moved to Leicester in the early 1960's, which is where she spent her childhood. But, it was in 'Shakespeare County,' Warwickshire, where she says she 'grew up' during and after completing her counselling diploma.

She is now an experienced counsellor, supervisor, & trainer, behavioral family therapist & author of self help books. She has three grown up children and eight grandchildren.

This is Linda's third self help book. The previous ones are "I shall wear purple" and "I shall be blue" which are becoming fast sellers and are currently available on Amazon.com. She is very passionate about developing both her own emotional growth, and assisting others in theirs.

This book is a dedication to all those who have substance misuse problems and those in recovery.

I shall be clean

Dedications:

<u>To my son Paul</u> - *I am so, so very proud of you and it is wonderful to have 'my little boy back' Keep up the good work. I love you forever - life means life.*

<u>To my girls Claire and Emma</u> - *I am so pleased you did good with your lives. Love you always*

<u>To my Grandchildren</u> - *I am so proud of you all*

<u>To my Mum, Dad</u> - *Family are what makes us who we are today. Thank you for making me who I am today.*

<u>To my work colleagues from substance misuse services</u> - *Thank you for all the knowledge and support over my ten years in service. And also thank you for those of you who have supported me in my writing.*

<u>And last but not least</u>

<u>To my clients</u> - *without which I would not have gained as much knowledge or insight into this field.*

I shall be clean

Other books by this author

Self help books:

I shall wear purple
I shall be blue
Teenagers are from Pluto

Counselling Text Books:

Introduction to counselling skills and theory
Training Manual for Certificate to Diploma in Therapeutic Counselling
Counselling and Psychotherapy Training – Level 4 & 5

Novels:

Jane me and myself
Gut Instinct
The Haymaker
A Woman's world

Children's Books

The Fairy on the Christmas Tree

I shall be clean

CONTENT

PROLOGUE

CHAPTER ONE	What, Why and the effects – *A little about drugs, there effects and ideas about why people use.*
CHAPTER TWO	Exploring your drug use – *An in depth look at why you may use, the groundwork for change*
CHAPTER THREE	Self esteem – *A look at the links between substance misuse and self esteem*
CHAPTER FOUR	Thoughts - *How your thoughts can trigger your use*
CHAPTER FIVE	Feelings – *managing painful emotions without substances*
CHAPTER SIX	Relaxation and Mindfulness – *Techniques to support your recovery*
CHAPTER SEVEN	Transactional Analysis – *A model of human behaviour giving an understanding and technique*
CHAPTER EIGHT	Early experiences – *how our early experiences can impact on us now and increase our substance misuse*
CHAPTER NINE	Ambivalence & Sabotage – *Strategies we will use to avoid change*
CHAPTER TEN	Parenting – *parenting as a drug user and the impact this can have on our children*
CHAPTER ELEVEN	Stopping and relapse Prevention – *Making a decision to stop and strategies to prevent relapse*
CHAPTER TWELVE	Parents of drug users – *Advice and support for parents and carers of drug users*

I shall be clean

Prologue

This is the third in the "I shall........." series of self help books. However this is the book that I have been looking forward to writing the most. Why have I left it until last you might ask - the only reason is that I wasn't so sure on the title - "I shall be clean." It almost insinuates that a drug user is 'dirty', when they are not. Never-the-less it took a lot of thinking about, and in the end I decided to go with it for the simple reason that this is the terminology that a lot of drug users use i.e. "I need to get clean" or "I've been clean for four months now", so realistically I knew that I would not be offending my readers.

I have worked in the substance misuse field as a therapist, couples counsellor and family behavioural therapist for ten years and I feel that I have learned a lot about this client group and addictions, both from my colleagues and from my clients.

It's very easy to get involved with drugs in this day and age, there is likely to be a 'dealer' within a mile of anyone's home. No matter what type of area you come from drugs are not defined by class.

It is extremely hard to come off drugs, once you are entrenched in them, by yourself. It takes motivation, willpower and it needs to be because you want to stop, not other people wanting you to stop.

Some people would define substance misuse as an illness, for me that is difficult to accept. Illnesses are things that happen to us that are out of our control. For example illnesses like diabetes, colds and flu, thyroid disorders and cancer. We don't ask for these illnesses, they just come. Whereas substance misuse is self inflicted, we choose

I shall be clean

to take drugs; we don't choose to get cancer. So maybe we could call it a self inflicted illness.

I do believe however that what maintains people's use is ill health i.e. emotional or psychological ill health and/or mental illness. Either due to life events/experiences, issues caused by their drug use or issues that were pre existing their drug use therefore they self medicate.

People take illicit drugs for all sorts of reasons, some of which I will be exploring in this book, but what I have learned most from my work with substance using clients is that for whatever reason they started taking drugs, i.e. to experiment, to manage painful emotions, to manage mental health problems, peer pressure and so on, they then continue to take them to obliterate the past, the shame, the guilt for starting drugs in the first place and for all the hurt that they feel that they have caused themselves and others. This then becomes a block to recovery, facing all the people who they have hurt can be pretty challenging when they are clean.

What I have also learned is that the media and society in general have a lack of empathy and can be quite judgemental about drug users. On the contrary they have been some of the nicest people that I have met.

My motivation for writing this book is that we are living in an age where therapy is becoming more and more difficult to access, waiting lists are far too long and 'brief' therapy appears to be the answer to everyone's problems, I learned during my own therapeutic journey both as a client and as a therapist many tools that can help us to begin to learn more about ourselves and change the 'things' that are impacting on our lives in a negative way.

Over the years I have collected many tools and have developed a rather large therapeutic toolbox. Some of these tools are my own and there are some that I am unsure where they came from, so please accept my apologies if I have used one given by you and not mentioned your name.

As in my previous books "I shall wear purple" and "I shall be blue" I wanted to share those tools with therapists and clients to

I shall be clean

support people in their struggle with substance misuse.

Although this book is by no means a tool to replace therapy, nothing can beat the process of a good therapeutic relationship and the excellent work that therapists worldwide do. Nor is it a tool to replace medical intervention, or the great work that drug workers do across the country.

It is a tool to start you on that journey, to give you an insight into different therapeutic models so that you can decide which therapeutic model feels the right one for you, (we are all different and what works for one, does not always work for another) and to give you an appreciation on what therapy is about, how it works and how it can change your life and the way that you function as a human being. This way you are in charge of your own treatment journey and can decide which treatment model will work best for you.

I hope that this book offers you the above and more.

Linda x

I shall be clean

CHAPTER ONE
What and Why?

I'm not going to spend too much time writing about the different illicit drugs available today; as if you are reading this book to help you to work towards recovery then I have no doubt that you probably know more about them than I do. If you are not a drug user then there is an abundance of information on the internet to research the drug that you may be concerned about.

I will however give a brief outline of commonly known drugs and the how they work.

Stimulants	Depressants	Hallucinogenics
Amphetamine	Cannabis	LSD
Ecstasy	Heroin	Magic mushrooms
Cocaine		
Crack		

Stimulants

First we will look at stimulants and how they work on the neurological system. Stimulants speed or stimulate the central nervous system. Stimulants give a sense of euphoria and this is due to the following:

Inside our brain we have a neurotransmitter (giver of pleasure) and a receptor a (receiver of pleasure). Each time we experience something good the neurotransmitter goes into the receptor releases some endorphins (happy bubbles) leaving you feeling a sense of euphoria and comes out again. Many things can do this, a party,

I shall be clean

Christmas coming, chocolate, sex etc.

Stimulants however stop the neurotransmitter from coming out of the receptor. It holds it in and releases a full load of endorphins. (Emptying you bubble bag). This is what gives the user a big high and a sense of euphoria.

This is why stimulant users experience a massive crash when they come down off the drug. They have no happy bubbles left and although they will rejuvenate it could take a couple of days to sometimes a month or so.

Depressants

Depressants are substances which slow down the normal function of the central nervous system. These drugs include barbiturates, benzodiazepines, and alcohol. Heroin, Marijuana and some inhalants are also depressants.

The use of depressants can result in a slowed pulse and breathing, slurred speech, drowsiness, lowered blood pressure, poor concentration, fatigue and confusion, as well as impaired coordination, memory and judgment.

Clients describe the experience of this drug as floating on a cloud, without a care in the world. A 'chilling out' that they cant get by any other means. All their problems disappear and they have a calming effect. Some clients have also experienced a sense of being out of control and not liking that actual sensation.

Prolonged or heavy abuse of depressants can result in addiction, impaired sexual function, chronic sleep problems, respiratory depression and in some cases, very thankfully not all respiratory arrest, and death.

Hallucinogenics

The term *hallucinogen* refers to a variety of substances capable of inducing profound altered states of consciousness; these substances have a long history of use in societies throughout the world.

I shall be clean

These substances induce a hyper-suggestible state to be general; hallucinogens are psychoactive drugs that produce altered perceptions or ways of thinking and feeling when taken.

Psychedelic drugs alter the way you perceive the world around you and are said to expand the mind, that is turn off your brain's selective perception function and allow you to perceive everything around you in a more intense and colourful way.

Mind and Body

Needless to say there are a lot of other drugs on the market, but I have covered the ones that from my experience most clients present with. All drugs are mind altering and although some people have a good experience on them there are many that have a bad experience on them.

There is no doubt about when you take an illicit drug you are messing with your mind and your body. Drugs can have short term and long term effects on users health and some drugs will mask physical pain which lets us know there is a problem with our bodies.

Although from my experience health, neither psychological nor physical is a strong motivation for users to change. Like most of us we never think it will happen to us. Never the less, I always share this information with them anyway.

I use an example similar to a cardiograph to clients to explain the way drugs work on our psychological and emotional wellbeing. First of all:

This is a six month life line of a non drug user:

This demonstrates the 'ups and downs' of life over a six month period.

I shall be clean

This is a six month life line of an amphetamine or cocaine user:

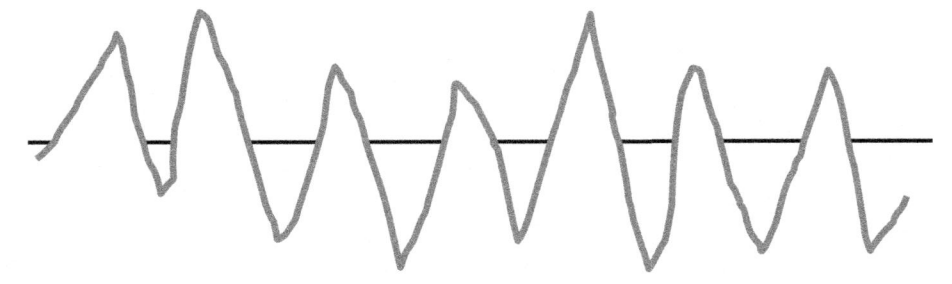

Showing the massive 'highs and lows' experienced by their drug use.

This is a six month life line of a crack user:

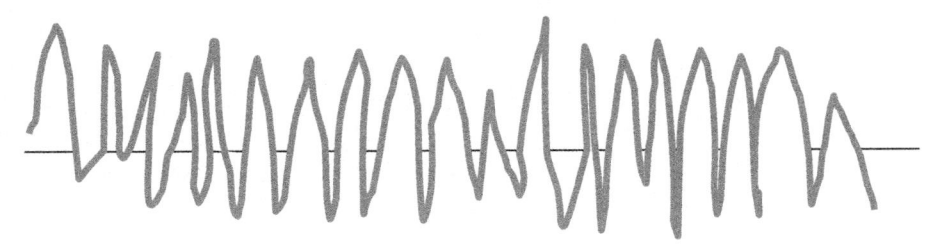

As you will notice the highs and lows are much more frequent and as with the cocaine and speed lifeline the lows become more frequent than the highs after a period of use.

And last but not least this is the 6 month life line of someone on a depressant:

They appear to not experience any of the natural highs and lows of life, and just plod along in their own little world. The problem with this is that those natural highs and lows are what help us to grow emotionally and psychologically.

I shall be clean

Imagine that I, a stimulant user and a depressant user went out and brought a top of the range motor car tomorrow:

The stimulant user was a boy racer. He used his car everyday on a racetrack and did speeds of up to 150 miles an hour.

The depressant user's car did not get used at all it was just left outside in all weathers.

However, I used my car to pop around town, and go to work usually going at about 30 to 50 miles an hour. Whose car would last the longest do you think?

Yes mine would!

That is because the boy racer would wear his out and the person on depressants car would just rot away. Stop working.

That is an analogy of what drugs can do to our bodies. Stimulants make the heart go faster. The heart controls the speed of every other organ in your body, so if your heart goes faster then so does your kidneys, liver etc. Therefore will your body pack up before mine?

Depressants however slow the heart down and too many depressants can make the heart stop.

To write about drugs and there effects could fill this book, equally there are new substances that people are taking hitting the streets regularly, from legal highs to zombie drugs, but I hope that I have given you a brief overview on some of the drugs on the street. More information can be obtained from the internet or a visit to your local drug services.

I shall be clean

Why do people use drugs?

There are many different theories of what causes people to become addicted to drugs, too many to mention in this book.

A recent documentary has just announced that from their own research they have learned that most drug addicts have a dopamine deficiency. I am unable to argue with research; however I struggle to understand why so many people in our society today then suffer with this deficiency? Or is it another 'which came first the chicken or the egg' concept - Is it the drugs that are causing such a high level of people with a dopamine deficiency, rather than the dopamine deficiency causing the huge substance misuse problems in our society today?

Being a therapist and not a doctor my experience lies with, the psychological/emotional causes of substance misuse problems in our society today. I will describe a theory that makes sense to me:

Emotional/psychological

Many years ago when illicit drugs were not on all our street corners, and the only time that we heard of them was that pop stars were taking them, or hippies in the 50's, we and our parents reached our teenage years with trepidation. These are the years when we felt at the time that our problems all began to get worse, from boyfriend problems, body and beauty anxieties, peer pressure, educational pressure, bullying at school, fitting in with the in crowd, and trying to break free from the control of our parents to name but a few.

It is also a time when we are flooded in emotions and that can at times seem unmanageable. It is a little like a rollercoaster ride. Our moods are up and down like a yoyo and there wasn't a week goes by that we didn't feel upset or angry about something.

We are very rarely taught good emotional regulation tools either at school or at home, so we learn them. We see how our parents manage their emotions, we watch how our peers regulate their

I shall be clean

emotions and this is where the problem starts. If you are into sports or dance then these activities will be good emotional regulation tools and we recognise that when participating in these activities we feel better. Unconsciously this is how we kept an emotional balance.

I believe that whatever coping strategy or emotional regulation tool that we come into contact with at that vulnerable age can stay with us for a long time. For example, some people find work regulates their emotions and so there is born the workaholic, for some it's gambling, or gaming. For others it may be cake and sweets and so on. We all need an emotional regulation tool whatever age we are, whether that be watching a good movie, reading a book, cleaning the house, playing on the computer, writing a book. When we do all these things we switch off from whatever is causing us pain, even for a short time. It give us respite.

However these days, if your emotions are turbulent, you can walk out of your front door and get any number of substances to make you feel better. A stimulant if your self esteem is low, a depressant if you want your anger to subside, an hallucinogenic if you want to escape into a different world. And so on.

It is my belief that this is how the habit starts when all those emotions are heightened and so then this becomes the users emotional regulation tool for many years until they learn healthier ways to manage them.

The problem is those emotions don't go away. When you are on your 'come down' they come back to haunt you and are twice as bad because now you have a hangover too. Then you may take more drugs to obliterate the present, until you are taking a lot of drugs on a regular basis to obliterate the present and the past and become an addict.

All those emotions then become suppressed and when you make a decision to give up for good, you stop and all those emotions come bubbling to the surface. They are overwhelming and unmanageable, everyday coping strategies are not enough to manage them and so it's back to the drugs to eradicate them again. That is one of the most common reasons that clients share of why

I shall be clean

giving up is difficult, and is why therapy can help you to do a slow reduction and help you to find skills to manage those emotions as they arise.

Trauma:

Often people will use drugs to manage the overwhelming emotions from an historical trauma such as abuse, rejection, abandonment, bereavement an accident etc.

Unfortunately, this does not help in the long term, it is a quick fix and you are only prolonging the agony and suppressing every other emotion, not dealing with everyday upset in the process, which again will result in a volcano eruption of emotions when you do decide to stop.

Therapy is the healthier option and a longer term result. You can usually access therapy in some rehabs, either individually or in groups and sometimes both, your substance misuse service may be able to offer you therapy or signpost you to the right therapy service for you. Alternatively you can access therapy through your GP or privately if you can afford it.

Mental health:

From my experience there is another group of people that are drawn to illicit drug use and these are people with mental health problems, which can range from depression and anxiety to bi-polar, personality disorders and schizophrenia.

Sometimes it is felt by mental health professionals that it is the substance that has caused the mental illness or in other cases these people are self medicating. There is no doubt that more and more young people are presenting to mental health services with serious mental health problems, so there may be some truth in the fact that for some people drugs can impact on your mental health in a serious way.

I shall be clean

But we will never know which came first 'the chicken or the egg' – until people stop using drugs we will not know for sure if the drugs are causing your mental health problems or the mental health problems are there anyway.

I would strongly advise anyone suffering from mental health problems to see a GP or Psychiatrist and get properly medicated, because what we do know is that although illicit drugs can have the effect initially of managing your problem short term, in the long term it just makes the problem worse.

Physical health:

In my experience I have met clients who use illicit drugs to manage physical pain too. i.e. back pain, arthritic pain and multiple sclerosis it is difficult to facilitate change with this client group as they believe that the drugs work, and they probably do, a lot of these drugs were used years ago as pain management. However, the problem is, the not knowing what dealers put in their 'gear.' They often pack it out with all sorts of weird concoctions, to make more money.

What I have also learned through my work is that drugs can mask physical health problems. Because they are a pain relief they could be suppressing physical pain that may lead to undetected serious illnesses, which if treated earlier could have resulted in a positive outcome.

The **National Institute on drug abuse** states that people take drugs for a number of reasons:

(a) To feel good – The euphoric effect
(b) To feel better – To manage stress/anxiety/depression
(c) To do better – To improve sports/school work etc
(d) Curiosity and social pressure – To impress friends

The problem with using drugs to self medicate whether that be

I shall be clean

for physical/emotional/psychological or psychiatric problems is that your drug use will inevitably increase over time because your tolerance to the drug changes. You will find that you need more of the drug to get the same effect, which can become very costly, much more expensive than prescription charges and/or therapy.

When people first use a drug they may perceive what seem to be positive effects. They also believe they can control their use. But drugs can easily take over a person's life. Over time other pleasurable activities become less pleasurable and the person has to take the drug just to feel 'normal'. They become addicted to the drug and then it becomes harder to manage life, emotions and mental health without them.

The term addiction is equivalent to a severe substance use disorder as defined by the Diagnostic and Statistical Manual of Mental Disorders – fifth edition (DSM-5 2013)

The moral of this story is that drugs are too easy to access these days and as a drug user once said to me "Linda, if I feel crap, whether that is emotionally or physically I can wait for treatment which can take up to two weeks or more sometimes or I can pop down the road and within minutes get something that will make me feel better straight away – so I take the easier option"

So I guess that until people want to change, are fed up with using illicit substances or the legal system does something about dealers then these illegal pharmacies will be more accessible than treatment services to some of these drug users.

If you have brought this book then I am hoping that you are ready to work towards change so I am hoping that you find the right skills and strategies to do this, and avoid the illegal drugstores that will only prolong your agony.

When you are considering working towards change, it is important to recognize the stages that we go through.

The following diagram will help you to see this. See if you can pinpoint where you are on this cycle in terms of your substance misuse.

I shall be clean

STAGES OF CHANGE

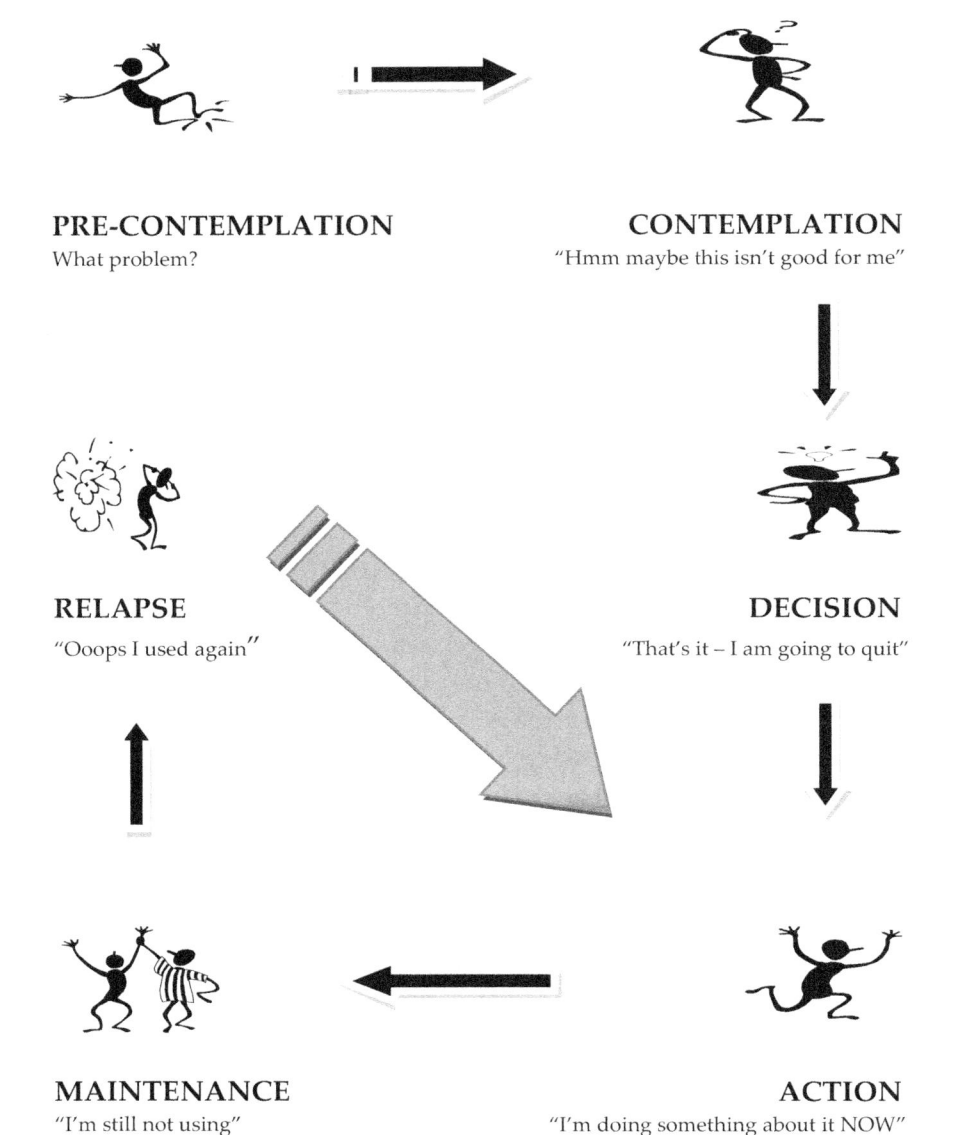

PRE-CONTEMPLATION
What problem?

CONTEMPLATION
"Hmm maybe this isn't good for me"

RELAPSE
"Ooops I used again"

DECISION
"That's it – I am going to quit"

MAINTENANCE
"I'm still not using"

ACTION
"I'm doing something about it NOW"

Notice the BIG arrow – If you do relapse then the positive is that

I shall be clean

you don't have to go right back to the beginning.

You already know that you have a problem; you've already recognised that this problem is not so good for you and you have already made the decision to change. Therefore it is just about taking action again.

Over the next few chapters I will be offering you skills/strategies to help you to manage the issues that arise for you when you stop using. I will help you to develop a toolbox for when you are ready to stop using drugs and maintain this healthy status.

It is important to bear in mind though that if your drug of choice is Heroin then you will most likely need medical intervention too, either a detoxification or substitute medication. This is because Heroin withdrawals are physical as well as psychological. I would recommend however that substitute medication only be a short term plan and you work at reducing this to enable you to be completely drug free. Substance misuse services will advise you on this.

And finally I would like to add at this point that I have not met a drug user yet that really 'wants to stay on drugs' also although it may feel difficult to become abstinent, those that have, have always reported to me that it was a lot easier than they thought it was going to be.

I shall be clean

CHAPTER TWO
Exploring drug use

My guess is that if you have brought this book or had it brought for you, then you have made the decision to quit or at least you are considering it well done!

As I discussed earlier in this book it is not easy to stop something that you have been dependent on for quite some time, what we need to do first is develop an understanding of the underlying issues to your dependency.

Often people just quit drugs without doing any preparation work before hand and this leaves them vulnerable to relapse. The problem then is that they feel a failure, which is another emotion that they will need to suppress and the more they fail the more this impacts on their self esteem and reinforces their beliefs that they are unable to stop. Then consequently increases their drug use.

However if this work is done first, then the risk of relapse is minimized. Everyone is unique and has their own reason for using and most importantly

YOU ARE THE EXPERT IN YOUR OWN DRUG USE!

Think about when building a house, what would happen if you didn't lay the foundations first? It would collapse. It is the same with your substance misuse, if the foundations (the exploration work) is not done first then it is highly likely that you will collapse (relapse).

That is why you will find that this chapter has a lot of exercises

I shall be clean

for you to do. It is really important that you do this part so that we get to lay the foundations to your recovery.

There are a number of tools that can help you to explore your drug use and so it might be helpful for you to work through them now.

Exercise One:

What I would like you to do is to spend about an hour thinking about all the reasons that you believe that you use drugs:

I Use Drugs because……………………

1…………………………………………………………

2…………………………………………………………

3…………………………………………………………

4…………………………………………………………

5…………………………………………………………

6…………………………………………………………

7…………………………………………………………

8…………………………………………………………

I shall be clean

Some examples may be this:

> **I use drugs**..
>
> 1. To manage my anger
> 2. To manage my stress
> 3. To feel good
> 4. Because I enjoy them
> 5. Because all my mates use them
> 6. To manage painful feelings or obsessive thoughts

Well done, once that you have done this I would like you to now take the role of your counsellor or drug worker and spend some time thinking and writing down solutions to the above:

Take the role of counsellor and offer solutions to the above

1. ....
2. ....
3. ....
4. ....
5. ....
6. ....

I shall be clean

Okay, your list may look something like this:

> 1. Buy a book, see a counsellor or join a group to learn about anger management
> 2. Buy a book, see a counsellor or join a group to learn about stress management
> 3. Explore what you mean about feeling good then find some alternative ways to enable you to feel good
> 4. What is it you enjoy about them, are there any negatives to that enjoyment and are there any other ways that you can enjoy yourself?
> 5. Are there any friends that don't use? Could you begin to spend some time with them? If not, how about finding out if any of your drug using friends are considering quitting, maybe you could stick together and do this as buddies and help each other.

If you have done this, **well done** you have begun to explore your drug use, and think about alternatives. This is your first step towards change.

You might find it helpful to start a journal, and write all these exercises in your journal so that you can revisit them. If you try and keep them in your head chances are you will lose them, keeping this information written down will be something you can look back on at a later day or something you can refer to if you are having a bad day and at risk of relapse.

Don't forget this is the foundations of your work. You are the expert in your own substance misuse.

Throughout the book I will be giving you some motivational quotes; they are a gift for your recovery. Hold on to them and recite them now and again, when you are feeling low.

Here is one for you now:

I shall be clean

> "Avoid looking forward or backward, and try to keep looking upward"

Exercise Two:

Now what I'd like you to do is make a list in your journal of all the things that happen that may increase your use:

Example:

1. When mum shouts at me
2. If I fall out with my girlfriend
3. If I get told off at school or work
4. When my friends take the Mickey

Bear in mind that I am not saying give up drugs yet if you don't feel ready. All I'm asking you to do is explore your reasons for use and if you decide that you are not ready then, you have the information recorded in your own journal for when you are ready.

You may want to take a break now. If you work through this book too quickly then you will not absorb your learning. Stop periodically to process what you understanding is of what you have written down in the previous exercises.

Think about this, if the washing machine breaks down, or your

I shall be clean

computer crashes, what do you do? I can almost guess right now what your answer was. Was it "Fix it!"

How can you fix it if you don't know what's wrong with it, what part it needs? Firstly what we do is 'Troubleshoot' – find out what the problem is, what the cause is and then fix it, otherwise we would end up going around in circles.

This is in a sense what we are doing now; we are troubleshooting your drug problem. Oh yes, there are plenty quick fixes out there that will help you right now, but that is exactly what they are quick fixes. Almost like putting a plaster on a 3" deep wound, the plaster will begin to come off and the wound will still be there.

We don't need a plaster right now. We need to fix this properly, so that you can lead a happy drug free life.

Exercise Three:

What I would like you to look at now are the positives and negatives of your use:

陽性 POSITIVES	無 NEGATIVES
It gives me confidence	The amount that it costs me
The damage that I think it is doing to my health

I shall be clean

Are there more negatives than positives, this is usually the case?
Copy this to your journal and keep it for later.
Now I would like you to explore the following.

Exercise Four:

What would your life be like without drugs?

Example:

> 1. Boring
> 2. I'd have no friends
> 3. I'd be angry or stressed all the time
> 4. Sad/depressed/anxious
> 5. I'd have no confidence

Again keep a record of this in your journal.

You know you are so worth more than this life you have chosen, you have so much to offer. You have many skills and qualities that you should be proud of. Think about a time before drugs, how did you manage then? Quite well I suspect. Think about someone famous who you admired when you were younger, someone of the same sex. Now write down all this persons qualities and the things that you admired about them. Describe his/her character.

Once you have done this, turn the page and write down all your qualities and your character. Compare this with your first list. I bet they are the same or similar. That is you, the person you are and the person you can again become. So the person you admire, you are the same as, so it's about time you started admiring yourself too.

I shall be clean

Usually and unconsciously we develop personalities based on someone we admired when we were younger, we take on a little piece of them.

Exercise Five:

Over the next few days I would like you to start doing a Drug diary. I am not saying stop using right at this minute as we need to explore your use in more depth:

When (Day/time)?	What were you thinking?	What were you feeling?	What were you doing?	Did it help?
Mon - 7p.m.	Life's crap	Stressed	Sat in my room	Temporarily

Looking back over your diary you may see some interesting things about your substance use. For example, do you always use alone or with the same people?

> Do you usually start using substances at the same time each day?

I shall be clean

- Is there a usual feeling (sadness, boredom, anxiety) that prompts you to use substances?
- What about what was around you at the time? Are the situations similar or different for you each time?
- What were you thinking? Did you have a craving or an urge to use or were you just bored?
- What substance did you use most frequently?
- How much did you spend.

Wow! Well done again. That's some exploration that you have now done. Go get a cup of tea and rest.

Triggers

A good initial plan for people who are starting off with changing their drug use is to avoid the risky situations and triggers. This may seem obvious but for example some people go to the pub after only a few days of not drinking and think that will-power alone will stop them from having a drink.

This is why it is important at this stage to explore your triggers to use.

It is important to remember that will-power alone does not work; you need a toolkit to manage the difficult situations that you might find yourself in. If you place yourself in a risky situation without the skills and tools to cope with the situation then you will frequently slip or relapse.

In the early stages of change, avoidance of obvious risks is important. For example avoid places where you used, the people who supplied you or you used with (if you can).

Avoidance is recommended while you develop the skills to manage these situations in the future. Avoidance is not recommended as a long-term plan through, as it is impossible for you to avoid triggers and risk all the time.

However, avoidance of a situation is possible but avoidance of feelings is not. So the chapter later in this book on managing your

I shall be clean

feelings may help you.

You may think that you are not very good at coping with difficult situations but EVERYBODY has a tool box full of coping strategies just sometimes they are mislaid.

Exercise Six:

What I would like you to do now is think about all your triggers to use and list them in the appropriate boxes below, this again may take some time but it is important that you try to think of as many things that may trigger you to use as you can.

These are both high and low risk situations:

BEHAVIOURAL - All the things that you 'do' that may trigger you to use:	EMOTIONAL - All the 'feelings' that you have that may trigger you to use:	COGNITIVE - All the 'thoughts' that may trigger you to use:
i.e. social withdrawal or watching TV.	i.e. Anger, Stress, depression	ie. "I'm worthless"

I shall be clean

VISUAL - All the things that you 'see' that may trigger you to use:	ENVIRONMENT - All the 'places' that you go that may trigger you to use:	SENSES - All the things that you 'hear, smell or taste' that may trigger you to use:
i.e. Dealers house, or paraphernalia	i.e. Pub, Park, Fred's house	i.e. Music, cannabis, coffee

Now I'd like you to spend some time doing the following:

1. Highlight the ones that you think are high risk

2. When you have done this, look at each individual trigger and brainstorm ways in which you can avoid or manage these triggers using the following sheet

You may want to avoid at first, but hopefully in time you will be able to manage them

TRIGGER	TO AVOID OR MANAGE
EXAMPLE: Stress	Bubble bath, go for a swim, meditate or read a book
EXAMPLE: Fred's House	Avoid for a while

I shall be clean

If you relapse don't beat yourself with a big stick, look at what triggered you and add it to your list

When you have managed a trigger (survived without using) don't discount this achievement, reward yourself, affirm yourself on how well you have done!!!!

WELL DONE!!! You have now got a clear idea of why you use, what increases your use, the negatives of your use, what life would be like without drugs and what patterns or themes are running through your use, and the triggers to your use.

1. "If we are facing in the right direction, all we have to do is keep on walking."

I shall be clean

So looking at the things that I have put in the exercises as examples this tells me:

That hypothetically I use when I am:

> Angry, stressed, depressed and bored
>
> I use to feel good and because I enjoy them and because all my mates use them
>
> I use to manage painful feelings or obsessive thoughts
>
> I find that my use increases when mum shouts at me, if I fall out with my girlfriend, if I get told off at school or work or when my friends take the mickey out of me.
>
> I feel that drugs also give me confidence even though they cost a lot of money and are damaging my health.
>
> I imagine life without drugs may be boring, I'd lose my friends and I would feel angry, stressed, sad depressed and anxious and that I would have no confidence.
>
> If I tried to stop then my triggers to relapse would be when I felt socially inept, angry, stressed or depressed. I would have to avoid the pub, the park and Fred's house for a while. I would have to avoid music, cannabis and coffee for a while too, and try to manage watching TV

If you have done all of this work you have also dipped into your tool box and thought about some ideas to manage some of the underlying issues to your drug use too:

I shall be clean

My example:

> 1. Buy a book, see a counsellor or join a group to learn about anger management
> 2. Buy a book, see a counsellor or join a group to learn about stress management
> 3. Explore what you mean about feeling good then find some alternative ways to enable you to feel good
> 4. What is it you enjoy about them, are there any negatives to that enjoyment and are there any other ways that you can enjoy yourself?
> 5. Are there any friends that don't use? Could you begin to spend some time with them? If not, how about finding out if any of your friends are considering quitting, maybe you could stick together and do this as buddies and help each other.
> 6. Explore some other ways to manage your emotions and thoughts i.e to manage stress have a bubble bath, go for a swim, meditate or read a book.

This exploration of your drug use is the foundations to change. You have gained quite a lot of information just by taking the time to do these exercises. I know you might think this will not help, that your urges to use are far too strong, but bear with me, after all what have you got to lose?

Are you surprised at some of your answers? Often when using drugs of any kind we do not think about why we are using, we just use. Now that you have some thoughts on your reasons for use, you may want to try and reduce your use. This will be at your own pace, this can be just a small reduction.

Remember you are driving this bus; you have your hands on the wheel and feet on the pedals. I am just giving you directions which

I shall be clean

you can take at your own pace and steer in the direction that works for you.

Tips:

If you feel ready to do this here are some tips:

Set some limits: Decide beforehand how much you are going to use and then stick to it. Try to make the limits reasonable and realistic, for you.

Take it slowly: Pace yourself, to rush at this point could lead to failure.

Start using later in the day: If you normally start at a certain time set that a little later, even if it is only half an hour later.

Eat: Have a good solid breakfast before you start using, as most drugs will suppress your appetite.

Keep yourself occupied: Boredom can be your worst enemy, when trying to give up or cut down and one of the main triggers to relapse.

Limit your spending: Decide how much you are going to spend on drugs daily or weekly and try to stick to this. Only have a certain amount of money on you at any one time. Keep a stamped addressed envelope in your possession every time you go out and if you have money on you and are tempted to buy drugs. Put the money in the envelope and pop it in the post to yourself.

Give yourself rewards for any success Get yourself some chocolate, new clothes or a magazine. Something you are going to enjoy that does not involve substances.

I shall be clean

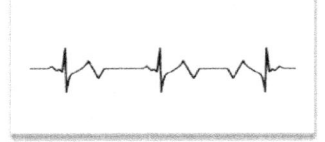

Already you are getting your heart functioning better!

If you are thinking about reducing, then it is always helpful to do yourself a reduction plan.

Here is an example of one for someone who smokes 10 joints daily. This will help you to see how a small reduction on a daily basis soon mounts up to a lot over the week and month.

Have a go at making your own reduction plan.

Example:

	MON	TUES	WED	THUR	FRI	SAT	SUN	Reduced by:
WK 1	10 Joints	9 joints	10 joints	8 Joints	9 joints	10 joints	8 joints	**6 joints**
WK 2	10 Joints	8 joints	9 joints	7 Joints	9 joints	9 joints	7 joints	**11 joints**
WK 3	9 Joints	8 joints	8 joints	7 Joints	8 joints	8 joints	6 joints	**16 joints**
WK 4	9 Joints	7 joints	7 joints	7 Joints	7 joints	7 joints	6 joints	**20 joints**
								53 joints

At a pound a joint that is a savings of £53.00 in a month by just making a small adjustment to your use. You can do this again when you are ready, but don't let your use increase again.

What you will probably find too is that whatever the underlying issue is to your use, this reduced amount will still manage your pain, your anger, your anxiety or stress and you will still feel comfortable.

I shall be clean

> "Success is the sum of small efforts, repeated day in and day out."

I shall be clean

CHAPTER THREE
Self esteem

Low self esteem has come to be seen as the cause for a wide range of personal and social problems, one of those being drug addictions.

For these reasons it seems important to include this in our work with drug users. And for drug users themselves to do some work around self esteem enhancement as part of their working towards abstinence, as this is supported by existing theory that self esteem does play a major role in an individual's use and abuse of alcohol and substances.

A commonly held belief by many researchers, teachers, school administrators, and health professionals is that "low self-esteem is associated with drug use and/or abuse" - (*Dielman, Campanelli, Shope, & Butchart, 1987; Dielman, Leech, Lorenger, & Horvath, 1984; Steffenhagen & Steffenhagen, 1985; Wright & Moore, 1982; Young, Werch, & Bakema, 1989*).

Individuals with high self esteem do appear to display a lower level of serious involvement with substances as well as a decreased tendency to experiment with them.

"Low self esteem is kind of the spark plug for self destructive behaviours, and drug use is one of these" – *says, Sociology professor John Taylor.* "It's a fundamental need to have a good sense of self. Without it, people may become unhappy with themselves, and that can lead to some very serious problems."

In my experience working as a therapist in substance misuse with issues of self esteem I recognised that drug using behaviour

I shall be clean

either triggered low self esteem or reinforced client's already existing low self esteem, which in turn created many other negative emotions.

Common emotions associated with low self esteem are sadness, anxiety, guilt, shame, humiliation, frustration and anger. Individuals may also feel chronically discouraged and demoralised. In extreme cases low self esteem can lead to serious depression and suicide.

Substance misuse often brings negative comments or criticism from significant others in your life leaving you with feelings of shame, guilt, anger, frustration etc., which then has a huge impact on your self worth. Often this will then impact on your self esteem and you may continue to take drugs to block out these negative feelings.

Critical comments from others, particularly parents is often down to their lack of knowledge about drugs and their own fears about what drugs are doing to you. Those around you act on one major emotion and that is 'FEAR' – They fear for your life and your future. This 'fear' then leads to 'ANGER' with themselves and you, anger that they cannot make you see sense, anger with themselves that they could not protect you from these drugs and anger with the dealers who provide you with these drugs. The feelings then shift to 'GUILT' – "where did I go wrong", "is it my fault", "if only I had listened more, talked more, allowed him to go on that school trip" – Blaming themselves for your choices. So your loved ones go through a multitude of feelings too, with no substances to manage their emotions. They go through the 'grieving process'. They grieve the loss of the 'YOU' before drugs.

If you can accept this then, you will see that they are not critical of you, they are critical of what they 'fear' you are doing to yourself. They are 'SCARED' of losing you. They miss you, the 'you' that you were before drugs.

Low self esteem is destructive. It can affect all aspects of our lives. It can contribute to our fear of rejection (which causes us to avoid closeness). It can make us respond to loved ones with anger and defensiveness, keep us from communicating our true feelings,

I shall be clean

keep us isolated, unable to be vulnerable, and affect our physical health.

Worse yet, a poor self image will feed a vicious circle. The very things we **do** because we feel worthless tend to make us less desirable to friends and family, thereby cutting us off from the warmth that we desperately seek. This cycle can spin a person into a deep depression

Therefore, **'Taking drugs because of feelings of worthlessness tends to make the individual less desirable to friends and family, thereby cutting them off from their warmth'** and so forth begins the cycle of using drugs to 'mask' the feelings borne of low self esteem, which then continues to create them.

Remember your drug using behaviour alone is likely to have created a low self esteem. I would like you to do another exercise for me:

Exercise Seven

Take a piece of A4 paper and put a line down the middle. On the left hand side I want you to write down five people that you admire, they can be friends, family, you can have one celebrity and you can have someone who is no longer with us.

Example:

<u>5 People that you admire</u>
Anne
Emma
Claire
Paul
Julia

I shall be clean

Now I would like you to write down on the right hand side three things that you admire about these people, however you cannot use the same quality twice:

Example:

5 people that you admire	What you admire about them
	Caring, straightforward, brave
Anne	Good sense of humour, empathic,
Emma	non-judgemental
Claire	Kind, helpful, chatty
Paul	Loyal, fun, spirited
Mick	Honest, laid back, calm

Tear the paper in half and put the left hand side in the bin. You now have your quality list in your hand.

"It is impossible to recognize these qualities in others unless you have them yourself!!!"

That's right. So you have these qualities too.

What I would like you to do now is to turn your quality list into a poster, make it as colorful as you wish and I need you to make several copies and put this around your home, on the fridge door, your wardrobe door, in your car if you have one and in the bathroom.

Each time that you're self esteem is low, and you feel like using I would like you to read this before you go out to score.

This is a tool to raise your self esteem and hopefully reduce your need to get drugs.

If this stops you using once today then that is wonderful. These are your own regulation tools for when you feel low or worthless.

I shall be clean

Here is my example:

> I AM…………..
>
> Caring
> Straight forward
> Brave
> Good sense of humour
> Empathic
> Non-judgemental
> Kind
> Helpful
> Chatty
> Loyal
> Fun
> Spirited
> Honest
> Laid-back
> Calm

You have just named fifteen qualities that you have. Well done! Get that poster put around the home. You can even ask your loved ones to add to this. What qualities do I have? They will be keen to tell you when they know it is part of the work you are doing to reduce and then abstain from drugs.

> "Nothing is impossible; the word itself says, 'I'm possible!'"

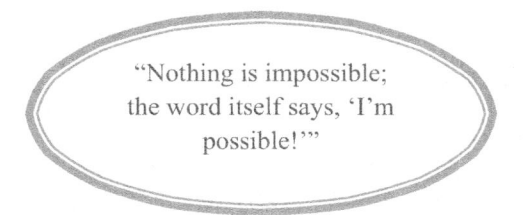

Often drug users see them self as 'just a drug user'. Sadly that is

I shall be clean

sometimes how others see you too, they and you can focus on just this one behaviour when there is more to you that just being a drug user.

Like this:

DRUG USER

YOU ARE NOT!!!!!

Using drugs is a behavior, and you have much more qualitative behaviour, as we have just learned.

The drugs you have been using are an emotional regulation tool, how can an emotional regulation tool be who you are. That would be like saying someone who works nonstop to avoid feelings is wholly a 'worker' with no other aspects to their personality.

There are many aspects to us, as you will have just seen from your quality list, all behaviours that are positive. As well as that we are parents, sisters, brothers, uncles, aunts, sons, daughters etc.

Your drug use is just a small part of who you are. NOT THE WHOLE OF YOU!

If you see your drug use as 'the whole of self' rather than a small part of 'self', this will decrease your self esteem.

Look at the following diagram. You could use your own quality list to do a pie chart like this:

I shall be clean

[Pie chart with segments labeled: Calm, Caring, Straightforward, Brave, Good sense of humour, Empathic, Drug user, Non judgemental, Kind, Helpful, Chatty, Loyal, Fun, Spirited, Honest, Laid back]

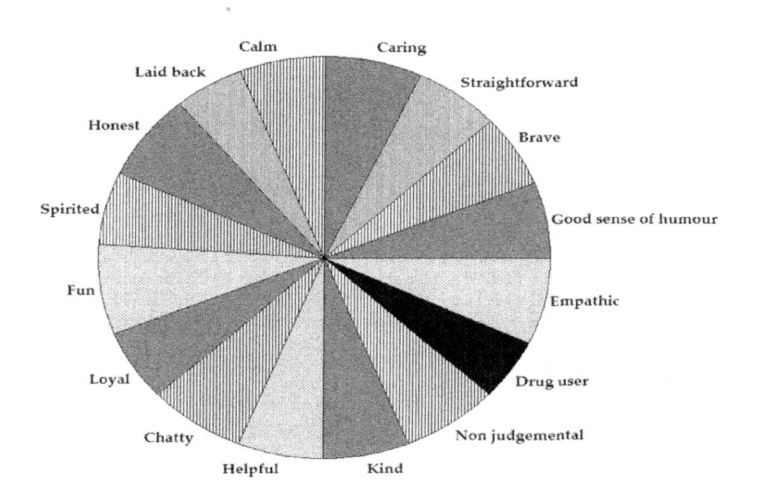

It is a helpful tool if you see yourself as the 'black sheep of the family' due to your drug using and drug using behaviour, and something you can show significant others in your life to remind them of who you are too.

Sometimes when you see your drug use as the 'whole of self' this not only affects your self esteem but also makes it difficult for you to change. Your thoughts may be something in the line of "Well I'm soiled, chipped now, so what's the point" or "I will always be seen as a drug user, so.............."

The fact that you were once a drug user should not have any impact on your future life and who you are. Some people go to University to gain knowledge, other's gain knowledge by life experience. Your past drug use has been a life experience, that you can learn from and take forward with you on your future journey. Think about what you have learned from this experience and what you can now do with that knowledge.

This tool enables you to see that there is much more to your personality than your drug use.

I shall be clean

CHAPTER FOUR
Thoughts

CBT - Cognitive behavioural Therapy is the evidenced based model for people suffering with substance misuse problems. CBT theorists would say that most of the 'bad feelings' we have come from negative thoughts or distortions, and that through identifying the lie behind the thought we can change the way that we feel.

The belief is that thinking, emotions and behaviours intertwine very closely and each can change the others.

When we talk about 'evidenced based' this means that there has been research into the treatment and the evidence has been high that this particular treatment model has been the most successful for this particular problem.

If you think about diabetes for example, diabetes is when the pancreas is not producing enough insulin which breaks down the sugar in peoples bodies.

Many years ago someone would have developed a formula that simulates insulin and there would have been tests to see if this was a successful treatment for people with diabetes. As it was successful then it becomes the evidence based model for treatment of diabetes.

In terms of substance misuse research, psychologists looked into addiction and it was recognised that people with addiction problems had a huge amount of negative thinking about themselves and the world, and as the belief is that 'our thinking impacts on the way that we are feeling', then working with our thoughts to change those feelings would be beneficial.

Experiments were completed and the evidence showed that by

I shall be clean

using this treatment model people were recovering from addictions. Although it is my belief that 'one model does not fit all' – and it is important to share that CBT therapists collate lots of information, whereas other models did not.

Many of the thoughts people have about taking substances are related to what people expect to happen to them while they use. These types of thoughts are called expectancies and are closely linked to why people use. **Some of the reasons people give for using drugs include:**

> Using drugs makes me feel outgoing and friendly
> I use because it's a habit
> It helps me relax
> Smoking cannabis makes me more creative
> I get better ideas when I am using
> I have an addictive personality
> It helps me sleep
> It gives me more confidence
> I couldn't leave the house without having a joint
> It helps with my anxiety
> It stops me getting stressed
> It stops me from being angry
> It manages my emotional pain
> It manages my physical pain
> Life is boring without drugs
> All my mates do it
> There is nothing else to do
> I can't stop
> It helps me to cope with life
> It helps me to work harder and longer
> Everyone hates me anyway
> My life has been so 'fucked up'
> Life is boring without drugs
> I like them

I shall be clean

It is very common, that our ideas about what a substance will do for us is not what really happens when we use. For example, a person who thinks drinking makes them more sociable in fact often feels more afraid of people and withdraws from them when they drink.

Someone who uses substances to manage anxiety is often very anxious when on substances, and even if they are not the withdrawal symptoms of some drugs i.e. crack can be extreme anxiety.

These thoughts are not always the truth, often we try to kid ourselves and make justifications for why we are using but again they are not always the truth. If you think in this way then it will be harder to stop. Let's look at how those thoughts may trigger you to use:

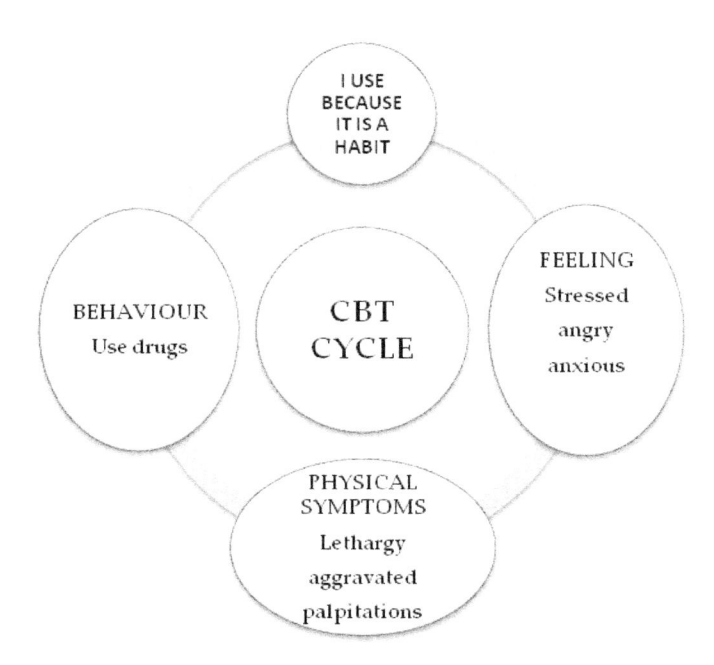

CBT CYCLE

- I USE BECAUSE IT IS A HABIT
- FEELING: Stressed, angry, anxious
- PHYSICAL SYMPTOMS: Lethargy, aggravated, palpitations
- BEHAVIOUR: Use drugs

Look back to exercise one at some of the reasons that you stated that you use. Try using this cycle to look at your drug use and reality test some of those thoughts. Be a detective and find the

I shall be clean

evidence to back up or dispute your 'truth.'

Do drugs really stop you from feeling stressed, angry, anxious, and depressed? No doubt you have said "Yes".

> "What lies behind us and what lies before us are tiny matters compared to what lies within us."

You are right they may do TEMPORARILY! They are a QUICK FIX. The relief is not for long and if you think about it some more you will find that although they give you temporary release, the feelings or thoughts that you have been running away from are back once the drug wears off and are usually twice as bad. The temporary relief is only supporting you in suppressing these thoughts and feelings. They never go away, they are stored until they come back and bite you on the bum again. These thoughts and feelings are there for a reason, they are there to help you to grow, emotionally and cognitively.

Do they really give you more confidence; do they really make you more creative? Get someone to video you when you are under the influence and then answer this question.

It is a habit, I have an addictive personality. Well habits can be broken and we can all be susceptible to having an addictive personality (if there is such a thing), never the less, we all have the ability to change the parts of ourselves, the parts of our personality that are unhealthy for us.

Also we are all prone to negative thoughts about ourselves and the world. When we have negative thoughts, they impact on the way that we feel both emotionally and physically which then influences how we behave.

If we are experiencing a lot of negative thoughts then we will

I shall be clean

feel pretty cranky. If we can change our thoughts then evidence shows that we can begin to feel better.

To change our negative thinking, which increase symptoms of stress/depression and anxiety <u>and</u> increases our need to use drugs, we need to start by looking at things from different angles. Just like when you want to buy something – say, a new dress or a house – we like to have some alternatives to choose from. This is the same with our thoughts; we need to try generating some alternatives.

If the video goes wrong, we troubleshoot. If our business is failing, we troubleshoot. How many of us actually troubleshoot our own lives. It's because of this that the same horrible things happen to us time and time again. We don't stop to ask why???

Let's troubleshoot now. Imagine you had the following belief:

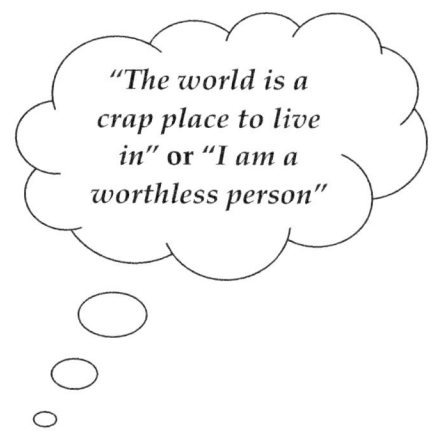

> *"The world is a crap place to live in" or "I am a worthless person"*

This belief could affect the way that you feel, the way that you behave and increases the symptoms underlying your drug use and most certainly slow down recovery.

Of course it is a LIE! The world is not always a crap place to live in and you are far from worthless!

Did you know that we have 30,000 thoughts a day and only five percent of them are the truth?

There are several risky thoughts when trying to give up substances. These are as follows:

I shall be clean

Risky thought	Alternative thought
"I can be with people using and stay sober"	"The risk is too great"
"I think I can control this"	"When have I ever been able to control this?"
"I won't let it get out of control"	"Why would this be any different than last time"
"This is more than I can handle"	"I can get through this a moment at a time"
"This will only get worse if I don't use"	"I can wait out an urge, relief is on its way"
"Resisting this craving is impossible"	"No craving is impossible to resist"
"It's free I can't pass this up"	"Using will cost me more than money"

These risky thoughts are all LIES! The alternative thought is the truth!

Let's look at what this cycle of the previous thought may create.

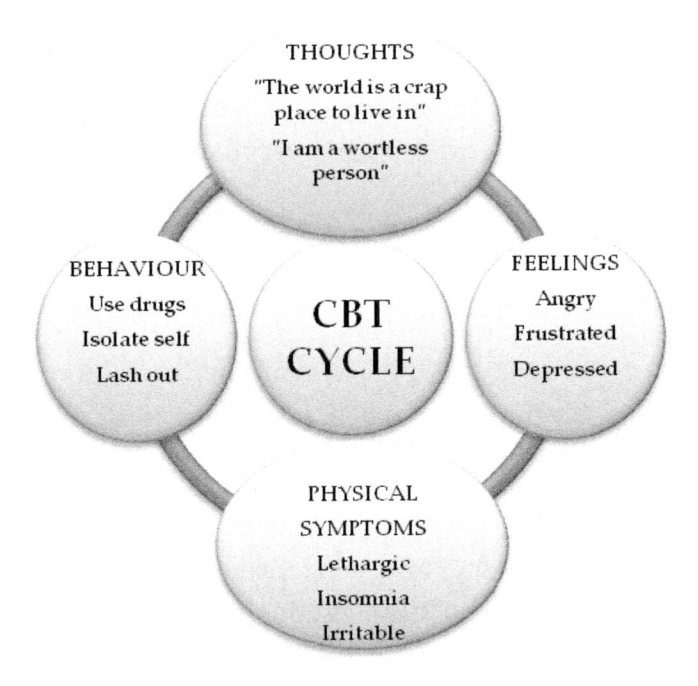

CBT CYCLE

- **THOUGHTS**: "The world is a crap place to live in" / "I am a wortless person"
- **FEELINGS**: Angry, Frustrated, Depressed
- **PHYSICAL SYMPTOMS**: Lethargic, Insomnia, Irritable
- **BEHAVIOUR**: Use drugs, Isolate self, Lash out

Your thoughts will trigger the 'negative' feelings,

I shall be clean

and subsequently your behaviour, which in turn may set you up for further pain.

They reinforce your 'negative' thought process. In other words 'wonky thinking' leads to 'wonky feelings' and these produce unhealthy behaviours.

Exercise Eight

What beliefs do you have? List some of your own negative thoughts. Now ask yourself: How helpful are these thoughts to you? How do they help or hinder your substance misuse problems?

Now check out if they are true? Where's the evidence? Ask yourself what would be a more useful thought or belief that is more realistic? What evidence or experiences do you have to support this new thought or belief?

Draw yourself a diagram like the above example and see what feelings, physical symptoms and behaviours that your thoughts trigger.

Ninety nine percent of the time evidence will show that your negative thoughts or beliefs to be a 'lie!' And yet these thoughts/beliefs, these 'lies' are affecting the way you feel, emotionally and physically and how you behave. They are not supporting of your recovery from substances

I shall be clean

Your life is what your thoughts make it

"Every experience in your life is being orchestrated to teach you something you need to know to move forward."

I shall be clean

Once you have reality tested your negative thought and sought out the truth, look what happens then. Look at the difference this new; more realistic thought would have on feelings, physical symptoms and behaviour:

```
        The world is a good place most
                of the time
        I have lots of fine qualities look
              at the list I
         wrote earlier in this book
```

BEHAVIOUR
Friendly
Sociable
Smiley/Open

cbt cycle

FEELINGS
Happy
Positive
Motivated

PHYSICAL SYMPTOMS
Energetic
Calm
Relaxed

Think about all your negative thoughts and practice changing them using this model, and notice how your feelings and behaviour change. Apart from helping you to develop healthier beliefs, it can be fun.

Everyone has inside of him a piece of good news. The good news is that you don't know how great you can be! How much you can love and be loved. What you can accomplish and what your potential is.

Doing these exercises alone is showing how great you can be,

I shall be clean

how much you value and love yourself and what you can accomplish.

I would now like to share with you my favorite tool to help you to challenge your negative thoughts.

Exercise Nine

You can use imagery for challenging your negative thoughts, firstly I need you to think about someone famous, this may be an actress, politician, sports personality or comedian that you really do not like, that you think talks a lot of rubbish (bear in mind this will be your perception).

If this person entered the room you would walk out, because nothing s/he said would be interesting, honest or make any sense. Everything this person says is usually a LIE!

Let's use mine and bear in mind, (I cannot use real celebrity's names in this book for obvious reasons, so I will use a pseudo name)

JANET POTTER

Now I'd like you to think of someone, who you admire and feel, talks a lot of sense. Someone whom you could sit and listen to for hours, and who is usually HONEST!

CHERYL COLLINS

Now choose your own.

The first person (*in my example Janet Potter*) is your negative thoughts, your critical self, you internal bully. The second person (*in*

I shall be clean

my example Cheryl Collins) is your positive thoughts, your nurturing self, the self that will challenge bullies, and challenge the things that are not the truth.

Now think about one of your negative thoughts, again I will use one of my own:

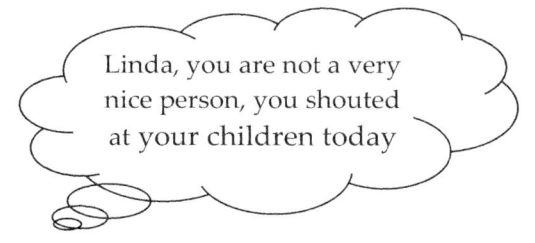

> Linda, you are not a very nice person, you shouted at your children today

Now say to yourself "NO this is (your bullying person) Janet Potter speaking, before I believe this I will ask what (your nurturing person) Cheryl Collins thinks, Cheryl says:

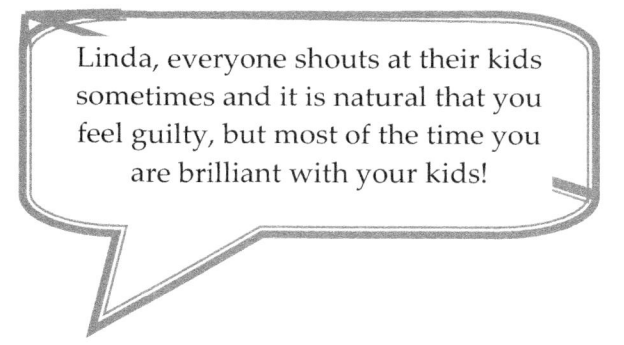

> Linda, everyone shouts at their kids sometimes and it is natural that you feel guilty, but most of the time you are brilliant with your kids!

Which thought should I listen to? Which thought is the truth? If I listened to 'Janet Potter' I would feel low, lethargic, and angry, disappointed all day and may even become depressed. If I listen to Cheryl then I will feel good, energised, motivated and calm.

It is quite clear which of these statements are the truth and yet most of us choose to listen to the lie, most of us will not challenge the lie.

Before listening and accepting what your first person has said ask

I shall be clean

yourself what the second person would say then make a choice which one is telling the truth and which one you want to listen to.

Let's face it if an external bully told you some of the things that you tell yourself you would tell them to "Bog Off!" – You can tell your internal bully to do the same.

We don't have to accept what our negative thinking (our internal bully) says, so stop listening to your internal bully!

In this exercise you could use animals instead of people, cartoon characters or any imagery that works for you.

A good idea is to print off several copies of your 'nurturing' person/animal and stick them on the fridge, your wardrobe door, your bathroom mirror, your desk, and in your car as a reminder to 'check out' that negative thought with your nurturing person before believing it.

The important thing is to believe in what your nurturing self says, this is the 'person' most likely to be telling the TRUTH!

If you are thinking more positive about yourself, then your self esteem will be good, and you will not feel so down on yourself and will need to use substances less.

Get into the habit of reversing negative thoughts. You might not even be aware that you are practicing negative thinking.

When you notice that negative thought or image is entering your mind, try actually to say "STOP!" to yourself. If you prefer you can use language that is stronger than 'stop.'

Another technique to stop those thoughts is to splash your face with cold water, or change your direction of thinking and sit and recite a poem or name all the pop singers with each letter of the alphabet.

By taking these steps on how to stop negative thoughts you will be able to break out of your negative thinking habits and replace any negative thinking with positive thoughts for a healthy and productive frame of mind.

Here are is another technique to challenge your thoughts:

Defusing Techniques

This tool I have found to be a good resource for clients who have overwhelming thoughts and/or feelings that stop them from being able to function on a healthy level. It is a mindfulness technique.

Defusing involves seeing thoughts and feelings for what they are (streams of words, passing sensations), not dangers or facts.

Exercise Ten

Identify the emotion you are feeling and/or label the unhelpful thoughts.

Is it:

- An evaluation
- A prediction
- A feeling or sensation
- A memory
- An unhelpful thinking habit

(An unhelpful thinking habit is when we do things like **mind read** – believing we know of what others are thinking, **negative filter** – only noticing the bad stuff, **emotional reasoning** – "I feel bad, so it must be bad", **catastrophising** – imaging the worst, listening to our internal critic).

I shall be clean

To do this we can use metaphors to help you to try to diffuse your thoughts and/or see things differently, here are some for you to try:

Passengers on the bus

You can be in the driving seat, whilst all the passengers (**thoughts**) are being critical or shouting directions. You can allow them to shout whilst concentrating on the road ahead, or even ask them to get off your bus.

Playground bully

Our thoughts can be our own internal bully. We can believe the bully (**thoughts**), get distressed and react from our emotions and the bully carries on. We can challenge the bully (**thoughts**) until the bully gives up. <u>OR</u> we can acknowledge the bully (**thoughts**) then ignore them and change the focus of our attention.

The River

Imagine your thoughts or feelings or images as items floating down the river – perhaps leaves or bits of mucky debris – instead of

I shall be clean

struggling to float, try standing back on the river bank and watch them all float away.

The Beach Ball

We try to stop thoughts – we hold the ball (**thoughts**) under water, but it keeps bobbing up. We can allow the ball (**thoughts**) to just float around us, just letting it be.

The Thought train

Imagine your thoughts, images or sensations as a train, watch the scenery (**thoughts, images, sensations**) go by, or imagine standing on the platform and watch the thought train pass by.

We don't have to jump on it (**hold on to them**)

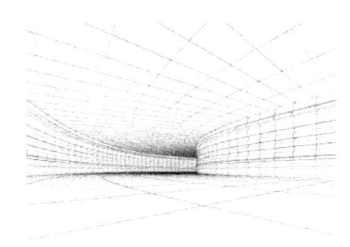

The Tunnel

When we get anxious driving through a tunnel, the best option is to keep going rather than try to escape. This feeling will pass – there is

I shall be clean

an end to this tunnel.

The Mountain

Whatever the weather, or whatever happens on the surface of the mountain – the mountain stands firm. Strong grounded permanent. **We can be like that mountain, observing thoughts, feelings, sensations, knowing inner stillness.**

Letting Go

We have 30,000 thoughts a day, however 95% are the same ones we had yesterday and a much smaller percentage are the truth, so let them go.

Make not your thoughts your prisons

Hanging on to unwanted thoughts can make you feel like a prisoner, they can deplete you of physical energy and from pursuing your goals.

I shall be clean

Leave the thoughts behind the bars and enjoy your freedom. You can do this with unwanted feelings too.

On this cycle we have looked at an exit point for any irrational thoughts. We also need to have exit points after the feeling, physical symptoms and behaviour too, just in case we 'miss' the thought, as follows:

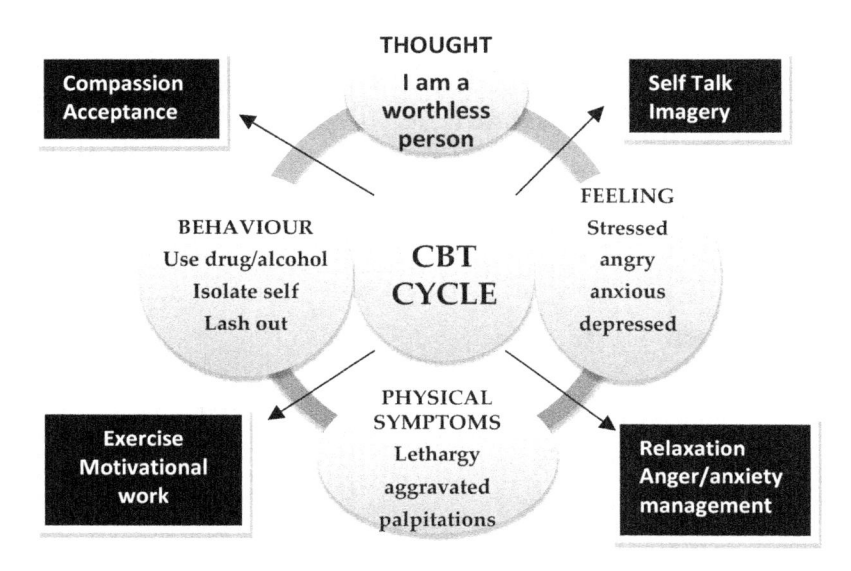

CBT CYCLE

- **THOUGHT**: I am a worthless person → Compassion, Acceptance
- **FEELING**: Stressed, angry, anxious, depressed → Self Talk, Imagery
- **PHYSICAL SYMPTOMS**: Lethargy, aggravated, palpitations → Relaxation, Anger/anxiety management
- **BEHAVIOUR**: Use drug/alcohol, Isolate self, Lash out → Exercise, Motivational work

So if you miss the thought that does not mean you have to go the whole cycle. You will have enough emotional regulation tools after reading the next chapter to use once the emotions kick in.

If the physical symptoms kick in then you will need something physical to manage these, and if you forget and go the whole cycle, then be compassionate with yourself. You are only human!

I hope this allows you to see that your thoughts and feelings are within your control and you are able to get respite from them, even though initially it may only be for a short while, the more you practice the above techniques the longer they will last.

I shall be clean

CHAPTER FIVE
Feelings

We have looked at thoughts and ways in which we can manage these, now perhaps we may visit 'feelings'. People run from them like they are a tsunami, however the tsunami catches them up in the end. If not now they will catch you eventually and the more you suppress the more you have to deal with at a later time. So we need to face them head on.

People often feel that taking drugs will help them to ease the feelings of sadness or depression, pain or anxiety. They think that it blots out past pain or trauma but the truth is it makes them worse in the long run.

People feel more depressed the day after using and often have to start again to feel better. An unhealthy cycle of using and psychological disorder occurs.

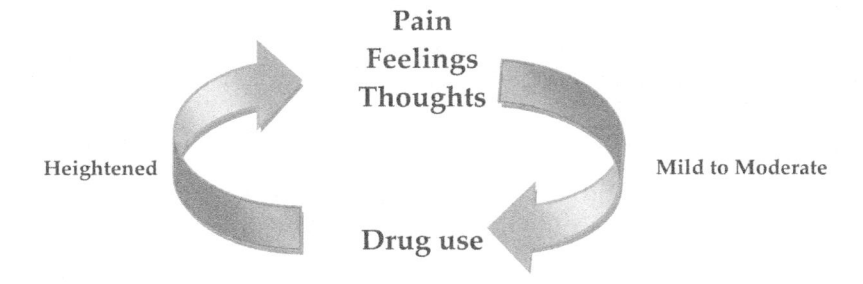

Pain
Feelings
Thoughts

Heightened   Mild to Moderate

Drug use

Many people assume that when they stop using drugs they'll automatically feel better about themselves and about their life in general. This is certainly true for the majority of people. They feel healthier, happier, more positive and more self-confident. They also

I shall be clean

have more energy to do things – and they enjoy their lives much more.

For some though things don't go quite as well. After stopping many people experience 'mood swings'. They feel OK and quite cheerful one day and then really miserable the next day. Feeling irritable, bad-tempered, argumentative and ratty are particularly common. Needless to say all this can make life difficult for you and those around you.

These mood swings are sometimes thought to be because the body is adjusting to the chemical changes caused by stopping taking drugs.

They may also be related to the need to find new ways of coping with the problems and difficulties of life, particularly if you started using drugs quite young you may not have developed enough coping strategies/emotional regulation tools.

The majority of people who experience these difficulties find that after a few weeks their mood gradually levels out. Occasionally however, a person's low mood can carry on. If this happens to you please speak to your GP about it. The underlying issues to your drug use may be depression, anxiety or any other mental illness that may need further treatment, therapy and/or medication.

When stopping stimulant use you may get feelings of deep anxiety. These feelings can be very frightening. They will go away it is a normal 'come down' from stimulant use, it is what we call the 'fight or flight syndrome.' As explained earlier in this book, your body is rejuvenating your 'happy bubbles' and this may take some time.

We will now look at some of the difficult feelings that you may experience and how to manage them.

1. Anxiety
2. Depression
3. Anger
4. Assertiveness
5. Perfectionism

I shall be clean

We will also look at rescuing behaviours. In my experience drug users are very caring people and want to help everyone else, the problem with this behaviour is that it usually back fires on us and leaves us with very painful emotions.

But first.............

Anxiety

Anxiety is a normal emotion. Without some level of anxiety we would not look left or right to cross the road or be cautious when walking alone at night, if we had no anxiety.

Anxiety is a multisystem response to a perceived threat or danger. It reflects a combination of biochemical changes in the body, your personal history and memory and the social situation.

It is perfectly normal to get anxiety when going to sit exams, going for a job interview or maybe even a first date, although uncomfortable we are rubber banding back to all the other exams/job interviews/first dates that have been unsuccessful and it is our bodies fear that this may happen again.

Anxiety is a fear for the future. This fear is not usually "what if I win the lottery tomorrow" it is usually a negative fear which may have been reinforced by events of the past.

When we are anxious although the feelings are in the present, there will be a link to the past and this will create a fear for the future. (Remember the future can be the next ten minutes, week or month)

For example:

(a) We have a job interview, we remember how we failed a previous job interview and this creates a fear of failing this job interview.

OR

I shall be clean

(b) We have experiences 'rejection' as a child and so each time we feel real or imagined 'rejection' then we experience anxiety. Why wouldn't we 'rejection' is and was painful.

Anxiety can be helpful as it is sometimes there to warn us, to prevent us from re-experiencing painful events from the past and it is sometimes important to listen to our bodies.

But sometimes it is unhelpful because it can be:

(i) Not a real feel fear but an imagined one
(ii) Set us up for failure i.e. fail a job interview because our anxiety stops us from thinking straight
(iii) Because just because 'this' happened in our past, does not mean it will happen again in our present or future

A past loss for example may create a fear of a future loss or a past failure may create a fear of a failure in the future. Anxiety is a fear and when your body picks up that you fear something it can go into 'fight, flight or freeze.'

This is because we were born with adrenal glands. When faced with a dinosaur or equally dangerous situation, our adrenal glands kick in and produce adrenalin to give us the energy/power to fight or run. You see this kick in when men lift a car off a baby, without this adrenalin they would never be able to do this.

Your body does not know what you fear, your brain sends a message to your body to say you face something scary and your body responds accordingly, even when your fear is 'what if I fail my driving test' a situation where you don't need to be high in adrenalin. Your body does not know whether you are facing a dinosaur or facing a job interview. So it is down to you to calm your body down and let it know that you are not in any immediate danger.

You may not know what that fear is, a good therapist will help you to explore this. However, it may just be a fear of coping with life without substances.

I shall be clean

The symptoms of anxiety are as follows:

> Heart racing
> Breathing gets faster
> Muscles tense
> Sweating
> Pupils dilate
> Butterflies
> Nausea
> Dry mouth
> Become more alert

What to do:

1. Pause, take a breath, don't react.
2. Do the relaxation exercises in chapter six
3. Put an elastic band on your wrist and prang it (you may have to do this several times when the anxiety comes back)
4. Take deep breaths – imagine you have a bubble wand in your hand, take a deep breath and blow the imaginary bubbles. (Or blow into a paper bag).
5. Distraction techniques
6. Challenging irrational thoughts
7. Tapping – (Try tapping just below the outside of your eye)
8. Self talk
9. Mindfulness and meditation
10. Bringing self back into the present (read a newspaper or something newsy on the internet)
11. Self care/nurturing
12. Rub your belly (or where you feel the anxiety sometimes the chest) and say "I will take care of you, I will protect you!"

Ask yourself:

> What am I reacting to?

I shall be clean

> What is it I think is going to happen?
> What is the worst that can happen?
> What is the best that can happen?
> What is most likely to happen?
> Am I getting things out of proportion?
> Am I underestimating my ability to cope?

Tell yourself:

> This is the withdrawals from my drug use.
> Nothing bad is going to happen
> It will pass

Depression

There are many different theories of what causes depression, far too many to mention in this book. These range from medical reasons, psychological reasons to behavioural issues. Finding out the cause of your depression can be a minefield, at a time when 'thinking' feels like one of the hardest things to do, when you are so besieged with feelings.

Below is a brief synopsis that describes some possible theories.

Medical causes:

A central nervous system disruption in serotonin, norepinephrine and dopamine are thought to be a direct cause of some cases of depression.

Also hormone changes may trigger depression. Hormone changes are seen in thyroid problems, menopause and in other conditions, therefore it is always advisable to have these checked out in the first instance. Your GP will be able to offer you a thyroid function test and test your hormone levels.

Your GP can also prescribe you with anti-depressants which will improve the way that you are feeling. Be mindful that these can take up to four weeks to kick in, and when you want to come off them you need to speak with your GP and he will arrange a reduction plan with you.

The reason that we have to reduce anti depressants slowly over a couple of months is that is some cases if feelings have not been resolved then these can come tumbling to the surface again once you stop taking them. Reducing them in a care planned way then your GP or therapist can monitor your mood and work with any unresolved feelings that come up.

Then there are the psychological/emotional triggers to depression:

Reactive depression:
This is when your depression is a reaction to a life event, stress, a trauma or a repeated sequence of negative events that go unresolved.

Major Depression:
You may hear your doctor call this 'major depressive disorder.' You might have this type if you feel depressed most of the time for most days of the week. Talk therapy will help and or anti depressants.

Bipolar disorder:
Someone with bipolar disorder, which is also sometimes called "manic depression," has mood episodes that range from extremes of high energy with an 'up' mood to 'low' depressive periods. When you are in the low phase you'll have the symptoms of major depression. Medication can help being your mood swings under control – such as mood stabilizers.

Psychotherapy can help and support you and your family.

Seasonal Affective Disorder (SAD)
This is a period of major depression that most often happens during the winter months, when the days grow short and you get

I shall be clean

less sunlight. It typically goes away in the spring and summer. If you have SAF, anti depressants can help, so can light therapy. You will need to sit in front of a special bright light box for about 15 to 30 minutes a day.

Psychotic depression:
People with psychotic depression have symptoms of major depression along with psychotic symptoms such as hallucinations, delusions and paranoia.

Peripartum (postpartum) depression:
This is sometimes know as post natal depression, women have major depression in the weeks and months after childbirth. Medication and therapy will help.

> "People can be more forgiving than you can imagine. But you have to forgive yourself. Let go of what's bitter and move on."

Only exploration can decipher the cause of your depression. One thing that we do know is that depression can happen to anyone, and evidence now shows that it can happen to one in four of us over our lifetimes.

Depression often goes together with other feelings such as guilt, shame, anger and anxiety. So don't be surprised if you are also experiencing these symptoms too. Being a therapist and not a doctor my experience lies with the psychological/emotional causes of depression. Therefore, I will describe two theories that make sense to me:

I shall be clean

I'd like you to think about three feelings that we may experience:

Depression ⇒✵✵✵✵✵ **Sadness** ⇒ **Anxiety**

Sadness is a 'here and now feeling' to something sad that you have seen or heard i.e. a friend's mother has died.

Sadness is a normal feeling that we can all experience in our lifetime and does not usually render us dysfunctional. However depression and anxiety can. These feelings can have a huge impact on our lives and prevent us from functioning healthily.

Depression is an unresolved feeling from the past.

If you think about when someone close dies for example, some people will go through the 'normal' grieving process, whereas others may become very depressed. This may indicate that they have some unresolved feeling i.e. anger, frustration, untold love for the deceased, hence why the bereft person may have become depressed.

The unresolved feeling may not necessarily be connected to someone who has died. It may be connected to someone from your past or present. It may be some unresolved pain with someone that you have not been able to address or resolve, a bully at school maybe, an old boyfriend or a parent.

Depression may be the result of an old wound being splattered open, such as Loss, rejection, abandonment or abuse. You may have a theme of 'rejection' through your life for example and another rejection has tipped you over the edge.

If you can imagine being cut on one of your arms at four years old and it didn't heal, you were then cut in the same place at seven, then at ten, then at fifteen and so on, this cut would never properly heal and so could leave you not going out, getting up even for fear of being cut in the same place again. It is natural that you are going to develop all sorts of behaviours to protect this wound.

I shall be clean

This is the same as a psychological wound only it is an invisible wound.

Depression may be the result of a trauma that has not been healed; it may be the result of many years of bottling up feelings such as hurt or anger. It may be due to the many masks that you wear to protect your vulnerabilities (See my book I shall wear purple).

It could be linked to psychological 'burn out' or 'compassion fatigue' due to being a natural rescuer, spending all your time on others with no 'self care'. (More on rescuing later in this chapter).

Or of course it may be linked to a recent event such as a relationship breakdown or a health issue. Exploration in therapy can help you to discover what may have been the trigger to your depression. People suffering with depression cannot always see the wood for the trees, a therapist on the outside looking in can help you to chop some of those trees down enabling you to see things more clearly. (See book "I shall be blue for more help).

If you feel that your depression is an unresolved feeling from the past, then the treatment may be to explore this with a therapist and work through some of these unresolved feelings. (We will look further into this in chapter eight).

Whatever your belief about depression, it is treatable and curable either with medication and/or therapy. But remember substances or alcohol is not the best treatment plan for depression, it makes the depression worse and the pain worse.

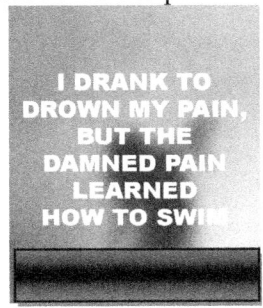

> I DRANK TO DROWN MY PAIN, BUT THE DAMNED PAIN LEARNED HOW TO SWIM

I shall be clean

Anger Management

As anger is a common underlying issue to some peoples drug use I have included some strategies to help you to manage anger:

Understanding your anger:

> ANGER is a feeling. It is not a forbidden feeling, nor a feeling that you should suppress.
> ANGER is not the same as 'losing your temper' nor is it the same as 'violence'
> LOSING YOUR TEMPER is destructive. It is to do with an outburst which is the outcome of frustration and helplessness.
> VIOLENCE is an outburst of accumulated unused energy. It is being out of control. It makes problems worse or creates extra ones!

Many of us are taught that 'violence' and 'loss of temper' is wrong, which is correct. The trouble is that we confuse these two with 'anger', so we also come to believe that 'anger' too is wrong and should be avoided. This we learn at a very early age.

Imagine that you are two years old and you are angry because mum has put milk in your bottle and you wanted orange juice. Or your big sister is playing with your favourite toy and won't let you have it.

We don't have the resources at two to say *"Hey mom, I'm angry with you right now as you have given me milk instead of orange. Can you change it please?"* or *"Please can I play with that toy when you are finished with it"* to your big sister.

So you throw the bottle across the room, the lid comes off and

I shall be clean

milk explodes all over mums new sofa. Whoops! Gee, mum's mad and gives you a big telling off or in some households a smack on the backside. Or you snatch the toy off your sister, she cries and you are put on the naughty step.

We soon learn that *"It is not okay to be angry around here"* so we grow up believing that 'anger' is a forbidden feeling. (However, we have actually got into trouble for the acts of violence or loss of temper – not our anger).

We then begin to suppress our anger, which can subsequently lead to a loss of temper or violence.

We are now adults, so is it time perhaps to reality test those 'early messages'. It is actually okay to be angry!

> TO BE ANGRY IS OKAY!
> IT IS A NORMAL FEELING TO BE EXPRESSED
>
> TO LOSE YOUR TEMPER OR BE VIOLENT IS NOT OKAY!
> IT IS A LOSS OF CONTROL AND LEAVES US POWERLESS

One way in which we learn to suppress our anger and release them in a loss of temper or in some cases violence is, what ERIC BERNE the founder of a psychotherapy model called 'Transactional Analysis' describes as "collecting trading stamps".

We will learn more about Transactional Analysis in chapter 7 of this book.

Eric Berne says that we collect stamps which are resentments that we suppress and store and then cash them in on others after a period of time.

For example: If you can imagine that you come into work each night and………………..

I shall be clean

Monday	Tuesday	Wednesday
Kids toys are all over the floor	Wife has broken your computer	Got a telling off from your boss

Thursday	Friday	Saturday
Dustbin men didn't take away your refuse	Missed out on a promotion	Neighbour comes to borrow lawn mower again

He gets the………………..

##!OUTBURST!##

YOUR NEIGHBOUR HAS GOT YOUR WEEKLY COLLECTION OF TRADING STAMPS!

Eric Berne says that once enough stamps are stored, we find a way to cash them in, on the excuse that we have earned the right to a free outburst!

How to deal with your anger in a healthy way:

The constructive way of dealing with anger is to deal with it in the 'here and now' (as and when it happens). In three steps:

I shall be clean

Feel the anger – this is to experience the anger. You may be in the habit of suppressing it, boxing it away in the back of your mind and not acknowledging this feeling and that is because it can sometimes feel uncomfortable. Find a space and some time (you don't have to respond to your feeling straight away) to acknowledge that you are feeling angry and allow yourself to feel the anger. Don't act on the emotion, which is a common thing to do.

Own the anger – be aware of what makes you angry. It is important to recognise that what makes you feel angry may not make everyone feel angry. We are all unique with different life experiences. (For example, someone who has experienced a lot of 'loss' in their lives may become extremely angry when they 'lose' something, whereas someone who has not may not feel anger at this experience). Therefore you need to own that this is <u>your</u> anger, linked to your uniqueness and your life experiences.

Use the anger – deal with the anger effectively, carefully, maturely and thoughtfully. When you feel angry (energy rising) try the following:

> **Try to stay calm and rational**
> **Think about why you are angry**
> **Think about who you are angry with**
> **Do you feel that your anger is justified?**
> **Decide if this anger needs to be released**

If the answer is 'yes' approach the person maturely and calmly

Own the feeling by using "I" (I feel angry because............)

Try to avoid the 'you' word ("You make me angry" will put the other person on the defence)

Use the person's behaviour rather than the person i.e.: "I'm feeling angry at the moment at these toys being left all over the

I shall be clean

floor"
Be willing to listen to what they say back to you

This way you are releasing the anger in an effective way that:-

> **The person is going to listen**
> **The person is going to understand what you are saying (people switch off to shouting)**
> **The person is less likely to lose his/her temper**
> **The person is more likely to negotiate**
> **The problem is more likely to be solved or a compromise made**
> **And last but not least, <u>YOU</u> will feel better, more in control and happier with the end results.**

Disarming anger – dealing with people that are angry with you:

This is a useful technique when you are in a highly charged situation and you want to try and reduce feelings of anger so that you can:-

> **Feel more comfortable**
> **Begin to listen**
> **Begin to start solving the problem**

It is also particularly useful when someone is telling you off, or is involved in a personal tirade against you. This helps you to manage other peoples anger with you in a healthy and constructive way.

This might be a boss, a friend, a parent or a figure of authority or even a mate:

I shall be clean

Firstly you recognise that this person is angry towards you and respond with: *"Okay I can see that you are angry"*

Then express your desire to solve the problem actively with: *"I want to here and understand what you have to say"* **or** *"I really want us to try and work this out"*

Get the angry person to lower their voice and to sit down, using a normal voice and calming approach: *"Let's sit down and talk about what's going on"*

Use active listening to hear all the complaints before moving on to trying to solve the problem: *"I can see how angry that must have made you feel"*

Whenever appropriate admit your own part in the problem: *"Yes I was being rather thoughtless/careless about that wasn't I?"* **or** *"I'm sorry that I made you feel that way"*

This way of approaching anger assumes you are willing to handle the problem and move beyond listening to try to resolve the conflict.

Simply placating the other person will only lead to further conflict, especially in the long run. So try not to sound patronising. Try to be genuine. Try to understand how the other person is feeling.

Remember that we are all different, we are all unique, and we all have different interpretations of things.

And lastly………………………………………

Taking out the heat:

I shall be clean

When you notice yourself becoming angry, there are a number of techniques you can use to 'take the heat out' of your anger:

Time out
Distract yourself
Watch a comedy
Relaxation or meditation
Self talk and positive thinking
Sport/Gym or a run

> One minute of anger takes away 60 seconds of happiness and peace and holding on to anger is like holding a piece of hot coal, the only one to get hurt is you!

Research is being done at the moment and evidence is beginning to come out that certain types of personalities tend to steer towards a certain type of drug.

Evidence is demonstrating that depressant users can often be:

Angry
Depressed
Anxious
In pain (physical or psychological)

I shall be clean

So manage this by using depressants. Whereas stimulant users can often be:

People Pleasers
Perfectionists
People who lean towards rescuing

Therefore I have included in this book some tips for people that feel that they meet this category and have this personality type:

Assertiveness

There a lot of self books out there for help with assertiveness, however here are a few tips to help you on your way.

There are many people who find it difficult to say NO when asked to do something. At some point in their life they have become conditioned to do what others ask, for any number of reasons. They feel that it is 'bad' to say 'No' or that they may be disliked, rejected, abandoned, not accepted if they say 'No' This is untrue.

Being assertive is asking for what you need, being able to state difficult feelings such as anger and disappointment and having an ability to negotiate well with others.

If you are a person who says YES when you really want to say NO, then you are likely to build up resentment towards the person who is placing you in this position. You then become angry with them, angry with yourself and if you suppress this anger then be sure at some point it may manifest into depression.

A friend once said to me "Linda don't do anything for anyone that you are going to resent at a later date." This was good advice because now if someone asks me to do something before responding I will ask myself "If you do this are you going to resent it at a later date" - If the answer is 'No' then I will say "Yes". If the answer is 'Yes' then I will say "No".

It is as simple as that, and it works for me. Why would I want

I shall be clean

to leave myself feeling angry and resentful?

I usually encourage clients who want to develop assertiveness skills to practice saying 'No' at least once a day. Even if they wouldn't mind doing the task asked. It will just get them used to the feeling of saying 'No'.

Remember that the object of our experience here is too maintain balance, to look after our own health first.

If you are unable to say 'no' and you build this resentment, it will result in you being out of balance which then can lead to illness

You don't have to say 'no' in an angry way. Simply say NO. Be sure they understand that you are serious and your mind will not be changed at a future time.

When you say 'no' to someone who is used to you being 'easy', make sure they know you are serious. Don't let them talk you around.

Be aware that they may think that you are simply tired, in a bad mood, feeling out-of-sorts at that moment and will reconsider and say 'yes' if they can knock you off balance.

When being assertiveness try following these steps:

Posture: When planning to be assertive with someone think about your posture, you can give away a lot without even opening your mouth. If you are crunched over, childlike then it is likely that whatever you say won't be taken seriously.

Eye contact: Try to look people in the eye. This can be hard for people who are naturally nervous or timid, but it shows people that you don't intend to be brushed off.

Calm, clear voice: Use a clear, calm voice. You don't need to be loud, but you do need to make yourself heard. If people aren't noticing you and you need service, say clearly "Excuse me." Also, whatever you are trying to say, try to be concise.

Say what's on your mind: Don't be silent if you have something

I shall be clean

to say. Share your feelings freely, it's your right. Remember, there's nothing wrong in having an opinion.

Learn to say "NO:" If you do not feel right doing something, then don't do it! No one has the right to make you do something you don't want. It's okay to reject someone. Remember, for yourself, the most important person is - you! If you don't respect your desires, how can you expect others to?

Be aware of personal space: Comfortable personal space is about arm's length from the other

Be as brief as possible: give a legitimate reason for your refusal, but avoid long elaborate explanations and justifications. Such excuses may be used by the other person to argue you out of your "no."

Think about the wording: "I won't" or "I've decided not to", rather than "I can't" or "I shouldn't". This emphasizes that you have made a choice.

Avoid feeling guilty: It is not up to you to solve other people's problems or make them happy.

Changing your mind: You can change your mind and say 'no' to a request that you originally said 'yes' to.

To be passive is to let others decide for you. To be aggressive is to decide for others. To be assertive is to decide for yourself, and to trust that there is enough, that you are enough.

Staying silent is a slow growing cancer to the soul and a trait of a true coward. There is nothing intelligent about 'not standing up for yourself.' You may not win every battle. However everyone will know what you stood for.

I shall be clean

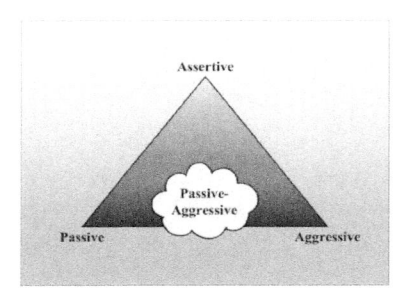

Perfectionism

Perfectionism is a myth

Perfectionism is an irrational belief that you and/or your environment must be perfect. It is trying too hard to be the best, to reach the ideal and to never make a mistake.

It is a belief that whatever you attempt in life must be done perfect with no deviation, mistakes, slip-ups or inconsistencies.

It is a habit that you may have developed from your childhood, which keeps you constantly alert to the imperfections, failings, and weakness in yourself and others.

Trying to be perfect at everything you do may result in depression as you will more than likely experience more failures than someone that is okay just being themselves. These failures will anger you, upset you and impact on your emotional health.

The underlying causes to perfectionism is often the fear of failure and fear of rejection, i.e., if I am not perfect I will fail and/or I will be rejected by others. This is a too stiff and moralistic outlook on life that does not allow for people to be human and mess up.

People who are perfectionist have the belief that no matter what you attempt it is never "good enough" to meet your own or others' expectations.

The wonky thoughts that play a part to perfectionism are that everything in life must be done to your level of perfection, which is often higher than anyone else's. And it is unacceptable to make a

I shall be clean

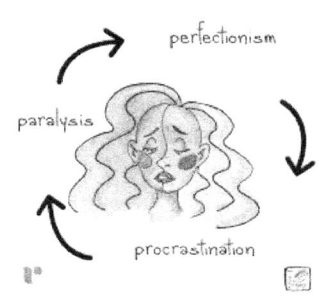

mistake.

perfectionism → procrastination → paralysis → (cycle)

The consequences of perfectionism are:

Low self esteem - because a perfectionist never feels 'good enough'

Guilt - because a perfectionist may feel a sense of shame for not achieving their own personal expectations

Pessimism - because a perfectionist can easily become discouraged or disheartened about being unable to reach a goal

Depression - because a perfectionist always needs to be perfect and when they can't be can become depressed

Rigidity - because a perfectionist needs to have everything in their life perfect which can lead them to be inflexible

Obsessive - perfectionists need an excessive amount of order/structure in their lives

Immobilization - because a perfectionist is often burdened with an extreme fear of failure, the person can become immobilized

Lack of motivation - believing that the goal of change will never be able to be ideally or perfectly achieved

I shall be clean

Anxiety – they will become anxious about starting a job in the event they cannot achieve perfectionism

Obsessive compulsive disorder – sometimes perfectionists may develop this

Stress – due to the high expectations they have of self and others

If this feels like you then here are some tips to overcome perfectionism:

Accept yourself as a human being

Forgive yourself for your mistakes or failings

Accept that the ideal is only a guideline or goal to be worked toward, not to be achieved 100 percent

Set realistic and flexible time frames for the achievement of a goal

Develop a sense of patience and try to reduce the need to "get it done yesterday"

Be easier on yourself; setting unrealistic or unreasonable goals or deadlines sets you up for failure

Recognize that a human being fails, has weakness, imperfections and mistakes; it is acceptable to be human

Recognize that it is OK to pick yourself up and start all over again

I shall be clean

Develop an ability to use "thought stopping" techniques whenever you find yourself mentally scolding yourself for not being "good enough"

Visualize reality as it will be for a human rather than for a super human

Learn to accept yourself the way you are; let go of the ideas of how you should be

Enjoy success and achievement with a healthy self-pride

Reward yourself for your progress, even when progress is slight or doesn't meet up to your expectations

Love yourself for who you are imperfections and all

Let go of rigid, moralistic judgments of yours and others performance and develop an open, compassionate understanding for the hard times, obstacles and temptations

Be flexible in setting goals and be willing to reassess your plan from time to time to keep things realistic

Realize that the important thing is to be going in a positive direction

    If you want to grow and improve yourself at all times, being imperfect is the only way, ask yourself why you want to be perfect and you may realize that you just want to be loved. Substitute that false belief with "the people who love me accept me for who I am not my perfection."
    A perfectionist is about desperately trying to stay in control of a world that is forever spinning out of your control.

I shall be clean

Realists know that perfection is impossible, and that every mark of imperfection has character, uniqueness, individuality. Most realists are striving to learn and to better themselves, not to achieve perfection.

Striving for excellence feels wonderful because you are trying your very best. Perfectionism feels terrible because your work is never quite good enough. Perfectionism is self abuse of the highest order.

Be kind to yourself you are a human being.

> I don't know the key to success but the key to failure is trying to please everybody.

Rescuing people

Take a few moments to think about your relationships. How many of them are you playing the role of 'rescuer?' Helping a mate out, saving a partner, and sorting family problems out? You will notice that you possibly go from one person in need of rescuing to another, riding into each person's life on a white horse to save the day. An understanding of the 'white knight' syndrome will help you achieve a greater awareness of your own compulsive rescuing behaviour.

The rescuer acts to stop people from feeling bad, to rescue people from some perceived harm or to prevent a situation becoming worse. They try to make people feel better. They try to solve other people's problems for them and become exhausted as energy gets tied up very quickly or you may become resentful.

Lastly it encourages a dependency; this is where the other

I shall be clean

person becomes dependent on you to sort out all their problems. Equally I will show you how it disempowers people from thinking, feeling and doing for themselves.

This is a tool for all those of you who tend to rescue people, then later in the day feel resentful or angry as they have not helped you, or not taken your advice.

I found this tool to be helpful in my own journey and feel very passionate about it as it helped me to change my own behaviour.

It is another tool from the theoretical model 'Transactional Analysis. This model will explore ways in which you can channel your empathy and altruism into healthy, balanced relationships:

Firstly I am going to show you the 'Drama Triangle' this is an unhealthy and unhelpful triangle to be on.

THE DRAMA TRIANGLE

PERSECUTOR

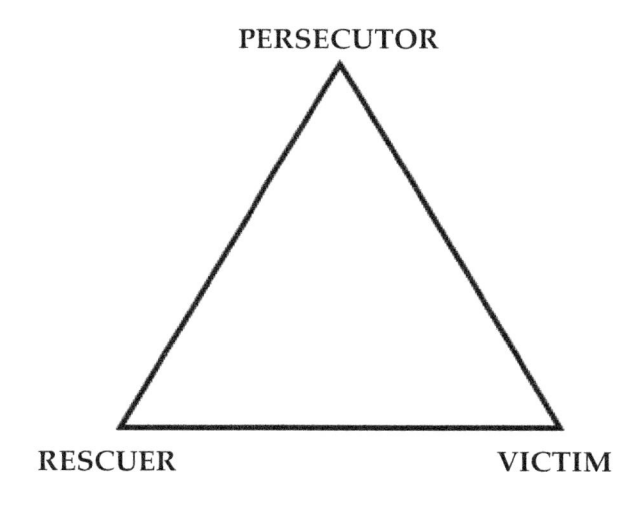

RESCUER   VICTIM

When people come to us with problems they are often in the 'victim' position and we can automatically go into rescuing, and this is often what they will hope we will do,

We rescue for lots of different reasons. For example:

I shall be clean

The pay off:- For a reward, to raise our own self esteem, so that they will be there for us when we have a problem.

To get rid of:- To sort out there problem so that they won't come back to us with the same issue, to allow us to get on with our own life/day/jobs, so they don't take up too much of our time/energy.

To feel needed:- Some of us have a need to be needed and if we don't can feel lonely.

To help us:- To avoid what is going on in our own lives and the uncomfortable thoughts and feeling associated with this.

When we rescue people we often do not get the above needs met. This is because often people just need to talk, and talk and talk, without actually doing anything about their problem.

Then what happens is we make a shift on the triangle. We may move to the **'persecutor'** because:

We feel that our advice has not been listened to.

We have spent the whole day with them, neglecting our own duties and they have not taken our advice.

We have sorted out their problem and they have still gone back to the same situation.

We may move to the **'victim'** because:

I shall be clean

We feel hurt that they haven't taken our advice/gone back to the same situation

We feel hurt because we have had a fight with them about ignoring our advice or using up our time and energy and made no change.

WHEN WE RESCUE PEOPLE WE DISEMPOWER THEM. WE TAKE AWAY THEIR OWN RESOURCES TO 'THINK, FEEL AND DO' FOR THEMSELVES.

However, let me now introduce you to the winner's triangle. The triangle that is healthier for you to be on, where you will feel better and conserve energy. Keeping yourself healthy:

WINNERS TRIANGLE

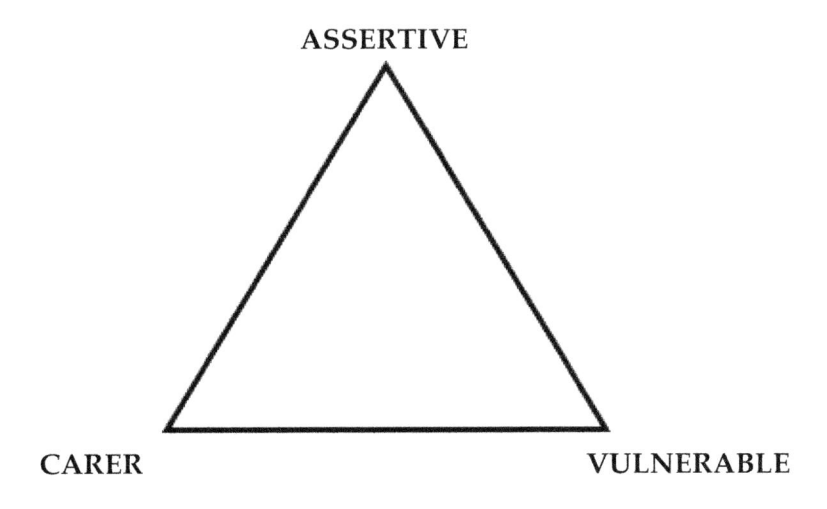

```
         ASSERTIVE
             △
            /  \
           /    \
          /      \
         /        \
        /          \
   CARER          VULNERABLE
```

When we are on the winner's triangle there is no shift. This is the healthy triangle.

I shall be clean

Often people say "I know I run around for everyone else, but I don't want to stop caring for people". **Well, you don't have to!**

Imagine this:

A friend or family member comes to you with a problem, you know that this friend might not take your advice and may spend the whole day complaining about their problem or the person that they perceive caused the problem. Whilst you spend all that time trying to rescue by giving advice or even running them around to try and solve the problem, you would be exhausted.

Instead you say "Gosh, I can see you are really upset" or "Gosh, that sounds awful" or any empathic response of your choice. Then you say "I can give you an hour to talk about this, but you know anything that can't be sorted in an hour cannot usually be sorted that day." So straight away you are taking care of **your** time and psychological energy.

When they have told you their 'story' you then say words to the effect of "What do you need to do about that, and how can I support you in your decision" – (needless to say we all communicate differently, so you may find a way to say this in a different way, however meaning the same). This way, you have:

Not jumped into advice giving or running around rescuing.

Not used up too much of your time and energy but still been caring and supportive.

Not held any resentments, anger or hurt because you have given advice or run around rescuing, and the person has not taken your advice.

AND if they have gone back to the same situation, then it is easier to accept as their choice.

I shall be clean

And last but not least it has:

EMPOWERED THIS PERSON TO THINK, FEEL AND DO FOR THEMSELVES.

> "Sometimes we motivate ourselves by thinking of what we want to become. Sometimes we motivate ourselves by thinking about who we don't ever want to be again."

Feelings

So, back to feelings:

When you are experiencing negative emotions, such as anger, shame, sadness, frustration etc, you will experience uncomfortable physical symptoms such as lethargy, sweating, butterflies in stomach, feeling nauseous etc.

Out of awareness you may then begin to behave in a negative way like using drugs or alcohol, lashing out at people, isolating yourself, etc. These are strategies that you will have developed over a period of time to help you to avoid what you are feeling both emotionally and physically.

We accept and stay with physical pain, but run as fast as we can from psychological pain as if it were a tsunami.

I shall be clean

By now you will have recognised that they are not healthy strategies, and they are not long lasting strategies, but they are strategies that help you to get respite from the overwhelming emotions that you may be experiencing. They have helped you to regulate your emotions.

As well as changing your thoughts as discussed in the previous chapter there are other techniques to help you change your feelings too, strategies which can help you to control your responses to overwhelming emotions.

It is natural that people will try to avoid their emotions and these tools you may already use either in awareness or out of your awareness.

Suppress them: We avoid them and do other things to avoid thinking about how we are feeling.

Cognitive Change; This involves regulating the emotion by changing the way we think about a situation.

Engage in them: This is not usually to process or troubleshoot how we are feeling but to help us to avoid another situation that we do not want to face. It is a way of control.

Adjust them: This is when we change a situation in our mind in order to avoid the negative emotion that this situation creates in us.

Attention exploitation: This is when we draw attention to something else rather than face what we are feeling.

These tools are what we all use or have the ability to use to avoid or manage painful emotions. They are our own 'Emotional regulation' tools and have possibly been useful strategies in the past.

Other more unhealthy tools that we may have used to regulate our emotions are:

Alcohol or drugs

I shall be clean

Gambling
Sex
Work
Violence
Self harm

And healthier ones but have their own risks

Computer games
Social networking
Various obsessions

DBT (Dialectal behavioural therapy) which is a therapy developed for people with Borderline personality disorders, have a lot of tools to help regulate emotions. I have found some of these tools helpful for people with substance misuse problems who are experiencing overwhelming emotions

One of these tools is called cognitive reappraisal. (correcting wonky thoughts), which is very much taught to you in the previous chapter.

Using reappraisal and the following strategies as a means of emotional regulation is more likely to leave you with more positive outcomes, such as experiences of positive emotion, social desirability and positive social interactions.

Whereas using suppression of these emotions or avoidance is more likely to result in negative outcomes, such as an outburst at a later date, physical illness and depression/anxiety.

Emotional regulation is using tools that can help us to change the way we feel.

Here are some strategies that you might find helpful.

Changing emotions:

You can only have one emotion at one time? For example you

I shall be clean

cannot feel happy when you are feeling sad, or content when you are feeling angry, or calm when you are feeling scared.

If you are feeling sad, try watching a comedy or horror to change your feeling. This works in the same way as when you have been feeling happy and you have watched a sad movie you then feel sad. Or likewise read a book of the opposite emotion.

If you are feeling depressed get active and do things that make you feel competent and self confident.

When overwhelmed, make a list of small steps or tasks you can do. Then do the first thing on the list, notice your change in mood as you do this.

If you are feeling angry, do something nice rather than mean or attacking. If you are angry with a person imagine sympathy and empathy for the other person. This will give you respite from your pain.

If you are feeling guilt or shame, say sorry – one word will be all it takes to change that feeling, guilt and shame is far more powerful a feeling than swollen pride.

If you have made a mistake then accept that it is okay, accept the consequences gracefully, then let it go

Behavioural strategies:

Sometimes doing something that makes you feel good is the best way to distract yourself from painful emotions.

There are lots of things that you can **'do'** to distract you from negative thoughts or feelings.

Here are just a few:

Wash the dishes
Make a phone call to someone nice
Clean your room or a room in the house
Help a friend with a project
Redecorate a room

I shall be clean

> Organise your books, cds, computer desktop
> Sit and write a to do list on things you want to do in your future
> Go get a haircut, manicure, pedicure, massage
> Mow the lawn
> Polish all your shoes
> Clean the bath tub
> Cook a nice meal
> Do a craft
> Play a sport
> Singing
> Window shopping
> Looking through magazines
> Make presents for friends
> Play music (upbeat music)
> Learn a language
> Complete a task you've been meaning to do
> Solve a crossword puzzle
> Re-arrange your room
> Invite friends over

Tick the ones that appeal to you and start doing them and add some of your own.

Distraction techniques:

Another great way to manage pain is to use distraction techniques:

> Distract yourself by paying attention to someone else
> Distract your thoughts with other memories or creative images
> Distract yourself by counting or using the alphabet to name pop groups, animals etc.
> Distract yourself by playing board/card games

I shall be clean

> Distract yourself by reading
> Distract yourself by doing a crossword, Sudoku, or word search

Interpersonal and effectiveness skills:

Relationships are precious, and they are vulnerable. Yet, sometimes in a matter of moments, they can become broken beyond repair. Keeping your relationships healthy and alive requires interpersonal skills that you can learn.

To do this you need to:

Develop good listening skills, and paying mindful attention to what is being said to you.
Develop good anger management skills.
Identify your own style of interacting and change anything that is Causing problems in your life.
Look at getting your needs met and meeting other people's needs in a fair way.
Strengthen your own self esteem and acting according to your own values.
Developing assertiveness skills.

Blocks to using interpersonal and effectiveness skills are:

Old habits – of the aggressive kind
Old habits of the passive kind
Overwhelming emotion
Failure to identify your needs
Fear
Unhealthy relationships
Myths

I shall be clean

Pleasant event strategies:

Sometimes doing something that makes you feel good is the best way to distract yourself from painful emotions. Try to do something pleasurable every day. Here are some examples:

>Organise a party
>Exercise
>Do yoga, tai chi or pilates
>Go for a long walk in the park or somewhere that is peaceful
>Go for swim or bike ride
>Sleep or take a nap
>Give your pet a bath
>Play video games
>Talk to a friend on the telephone
>Watch television
>Sleep or take a nap
>Get out of the house, even if you just sit outside
>Eat chocolate, ice cream or something that you really like
>Paint your nails or do yourself a facial
>Write a nice poem
>Draw a picture
>Laugh
>Wear something that feels good
>Have a rest during the day
>People watch

It is important at some stage of your recovery to feel your emotions, especially the painful ones, to enable you to get through them.

So when you feel ready and experience a feeling of being emotionally out of control, especially if you usually deal with being upset by pretending that nothing's wrong, consider changing your tactics and giving your emotions a few minutes of your undivided attention.

I shall be clean

Remember to observe your positive feelings too. Here is one way that you can do this:

Every morning ask yourself the following questions:

> **Who or what in my life makes me feel happiest?**
> **Who or what makes me feel most loved?**
> **Who or what makes me feel richest?**
> **Who or what makes me feel most passionate?**
> **What makes me feel most empowered?**

This forces you to go into a positive state, as when you are thinking about what really makes you happy, making the colours brighter, sounds louder and feelings stronger, by the time you have asked each question, your outlook will change for the better.

Okay. Over the last few chapters you have read a selection of tools that you can use to help you with your recovery so it might be helpful now to put some of them into practice.

I shall be clean

CHAPTER SIX
Holistic Therapies

You may find holistic therapies helpful in your recovery. I have listed a few for you to consider and access if you think they may be helpful to you:

Counselling:

Counselling is a talking treatment and all forms of psychological therapy can be called counselling, ranging from simple supportive listening to complex therapy.

Counselling offers clients a confidential secure space in which to confront, change or channel feelings of confusion, grief, rage or depression. The majority of counsellors do not advise or tell you what to do but help you find answers within yourself.

Other counselling services deal with things like addictions, sexual dysfunctions, moral problems or the wish to enhance the meaning of life.

Counselling is NOT a soft option but hard work for all concerned, They challenge assumptions and offer 'tough love' as well as understanding and kindness.

Counselling can help you to explore and work through the underlying issues to your substance misuse in a sensitive and non-judgmental way.

Auricular Acupuncture:

It is recognized that auricular acupuncture treatment is very

I shall be clean

successful in treating substance misuse, in both acute and chronic cases. It works on five points in the ear that represent:

> The Lungs
> The Liver
> Kidneys
> Pain relief
> Relaxation
> Cravings

This method tonifies the kidneys, liver and lungs which is naturally helping the body to detox more rapidly and strengthens your ability to function better and prevent further damage from the substances that you have taken.

The pain relief and relaxation points are known to have very powerful analgesic properties, therefore when tonified will calm and relax you and relieve pain.

The analgesic properties of these two points will also help combat cravings and withdrawal symptoms by releasing natural endorphins into the bloodstream which then replace the narcotic substance.

Acupuncture is also helpful if you are having trouble sleeping.

Reiki:

Reiki is a Japanese technique for stress reduction and relaxation that also promotes healing.

It is administered by "laying on hands" and is based on the idea that an unseen "life force energy" flows through us and is what causes us to be alive. If one's "life force energy" is low, then we are more likely to get sick or feel stress, and if it is high, we are more capable of being happy and healthy.

There is evidence that Reiki eases the physical aches and pains which are side effects of the withdrawal process. Furthermore it has been proved to be calming and soothing which helps a client to relax

I shall be clean

and sleep better.

Reiki has also been deemed beneficial for stimulant users whose brains are usually racing at a million miles an hour. It helps to calm the body and the mind down.

The process of Reiki can sometimes lead to resolution of existing unresolved issues.

Relaxation/meditation:

Relaxation & meditation techniques are becoming more and more popular and are a great help for people suffering with substance misuse problems and underlying issues.

Relaxation allows physical and emotional tension to be released. Learning to relax can take a while to master but the more that you do it, the easier it becomes.

There are a lot of DVD's on the market today to help you to do this. My personal favourites are 'guided imagery' or 'guided meditation' which talk you through the breathing techniques as you relax. They are available in some music stores and on some mobile phone and tablet apps.

Ensure that you are sitting in a comfortable place, a chair or lying on the bed.

Put your arms by your side and rest them on your lap

Put your legs and feet in front of you, uncrossed

Unclench your fists

Let your shoulders relax and drop

Feel your face relax

Close your eyes and concentrate on your breathing

I shall be clean

Taking inward breathes through your nose and outward breaths through your mouth.

Feel your tummy rise as you take your inward breathes and relax on your outward breaths.

Your body loosens each time that you breathe out.

Think of a relaxing word, such as 'calm' or 'peace' and say it to yourself every time you breathe out

Continue doing this for about ten minutes, concentrating on your breathing saying your relaxing word as you breathe out

When you have finished let yourself become aware of your surroundings slowly

End this period of relaxation slowly, in your own time

Take this feeling of calm, peace and relaxation with you into your next activity.

Mindfulness:

Mindfulness has been around for thousands of years. It comes from the Buddhist religion and is a technique that gives you the ability to be aware of your thoughts, emotions, physical sensations and actions, in the present moment, without judging or criticising yourself or your experience and without fighting or denying what is happening to you right now.

Mindfulness is known as 'observing self.' We very rarely do this; we may observe the 'physical self' - our body and the 'thinking self' - our mind, at separate times. The 'observing self' is able to observe both our physical self and our thinking self.

I shall be clean

It is the part of us that is aware of everything. We are aware of every thought, every feeling, everything that we hear, see, taste, do and touch.

Have you heard the saying,

"Be mindful of what's happening to you"

This is something we rarely do and yet to stay in that moment can learn us a lot, it can learn us a lot about why we are feeling what we are feeling, what was the trigger to my drug use, what am I carrying around with me, are there any feelings that are unresolved, am I talking negatively to myself, am I too critical of myself. Are my expectations of myself too high?

Being mindful of what is happening to you is not though about questioning yourself or interrogating yourself. The answers will come when you least expect them.

In order for you to be fully aware of how you are feeling, it's necessary that you do so without criticising yourself, your situation, or other people. Be completely accepting of yourself.

Staying with the moment means to tolerate the emotions without judging them or trying to change them. It means to completely focus on what is happening right now. The change will happen gradually all on its own.

Mindfulness is the ability to be aware of your thoughts, emotions, physical sensations and actions – in the present moment. Mindfulness helps us to distance ourselves from unhelpful thoughts, reactions and sensations.

If this sounds like it will work for you, a lot of CBT therapists and acceptance and commitment therapists use this within their work.

Here is a mindfulness metaphor for people with a dependency on Heroin:

OPIOID SUBSTITUTION

I shall be clean

People get into Heroin or Morphine for all kinds of reasons. However the journey is usually the same.

Let's compare it to getting into boating. At first you are given free rides and you like it. Then you get your own boat and you enjoy your trips. But soon you find yourself adrift at sea attacked by pirates.

You have to seek shelter in a shark infested area, full of reefs, sandbanks, rocks and dangerous currents and things get really unpleasant and very scary.

The sensible thing to do now is to throw in your anchor (get on a methadone substitution programme). You will then still be in the same territory but for now you will have steadied the boat and you are safe from running aground, drowning or being eaten by sharks.

Remember at this point there is nothing wrong with that sea anchor (methadone). Lifting it (i.e. reducing or stopping the methadone) will not by itself be of benefit to you.

You are not making any progress by setting yourself adrift again in those dangerous waters.

I shall be clean

In the distance you will see land and you will want to head towards it (move on). So you think about where to go from here, looking for a safe direction and a worthwhile goal.

At some time your anchor has turned into a hindrance and lifting it (i.e. getting off the methadone) will set you free to move towards the goals you have chosen according to your deeply held values.

This is where your key worker, the doctor, the CDT counsellor or psychologist can help you. Once you have made up your mind where you want to go, you plot a course out of the treacherous waters. And reach that dry land!

The important thing is for you to take good care of yourself, you are recovering from substance misuse and your body will be adjusting to the lack of chemicals that you have been putting in your body so it will take some time to feel one hundred percent well again.

But you will get well again!

| I shall be clean

CHAPTER SEVEN
Transactional Analysis

Transaction analysis was founded by Eric Berne. It is model of therapy that helps us to analysis our own transactions and enables us to explore why sometimes they cause more problems than good.

The theory of transactional analysis is that we all have three parts which Eric Berne calls ego states. We have a parent ego-state, an adult ego state and a child ego state.

This is the diagram of the ego state model.

Ego state model

P

A

C

I shall be clean

Eric Berne believes that we move in and out of these states during our daily lives and during various situations, feelings and thoughts. (Different transactions)

Up until now this has probably been 'out of your awareness', however learning about ego-states enables us to bring this into 'our awareness', which can help you to form healthier relationships and think and behave in healthy ways.

During any transaction when we are in our parent ego state, we feel, think and behave as our own parents or caretakers did.

This is where our transactions could be critical or nurturing, both externally and internally.

When we are in our child ego state we feel, think and behave as we did as children, although sometimes in a more adult way. This is the state we may be in when our transactions are sulky and argumentative.

However, when we are in our adult ego state we behave in a more constructive fashion.

This is when we do our reality testing and logical thinking. This is where we challenge our 'wonky thinking' discussed earlier in this book. In adult we deal with situations in the 'here and now' without letting past or future issues cloud our judgement.

When we buy and take drugs we are in our child ego state, to explain why look at this:

"I want drugs now!" "Oh no! You must not!" "The cravings will pass"

It is the Child ego state that what things instantly even if it means stealing it. The Parent ego state will say 'that is bad and that you are bad' and the a Adult ego state, that will say you're your money in a self addressed envelope, the feeling will pass' This all happens internally.

I shall be clean

It will be helpful if you spend some time analysing which ego state that you are in at different times of the day and in different situations. This brings you to more awareness of ego states.

One of the common mistakes when people are doing this work is to confuse their parent ego state with their adult. That is okay it takes a while.

The more that you practice and incorporate this into your daily lives, the better at it you will become. Remember all ego states are healthy when in the right one at the right time.

To help you along the way, here are a few tips:

CHILD EGO STATE is when we are hurting, sulking, fighting, arguing, or hurting other people.

It is when we are throwing tantrums, slamming doors, acting the goat, playing psychological games, or being the victim.

It is when we are unassertive, people pleasing, have a low self-esteem, embarrassed, feeling good, silly, and bad, bullying, teasing and joking. It is all the things we did, as children so be it sometimes in an adult way.

This is the ego-state that a dealer will try to hook, when selling you drugs. It is a technique sales men will use to get people to buy their products, and let's face it that is what dealers are, unscrupulous sales people trying to get your money so that they can have new cars and holidays.

It is also where you carry all your own emotions, and where some people will try to hook, the minute that they hook into this, you have lost the battle! Because you will more than likely throw a tantrum just as you did as a kid or lose control.

When you are in your Child ego state you are likely to be responding to a situation or stimulus using thoughts, feelings and behaviours from the past. It is not always negative; when you are

I shall be clean

larking about with your mates it is positive. It's good to be in Child sometimes when having safe, healthy fun.

PARENT EGO STATE is when we are scolding, criticising, praising, dictating, persecuting, teaching, nursing or nurturing self and others.

It is all the things we can remember our own caretakers doing. Remember that we will have a critical parent and a positive parent. This can be internally or externally. Be mindful that our dictating parent ego state can come out too when in conflict, so that's not helpful either.

We do have to be in our parent ego state when nurturing, setting clear boundaries and consequences.

It is our internal Parent ego state that reminds us to look left and right before crossing the road. It holds all the feelings and behaviours learned from our external parents and caretakers. It is what causes us to be self critical and what we can pull out to be self nurturing.

ADULT EGO STATE is when we are calm, rational, thinking logically and reality testing.

It is when we deal with our own and others emotions constructively.

It is when we are comfortable, okay, non judgmental accepting and honest. It is the ego state we often try to stay in, in our work environment.

The adult ego state is the ego state that helps you to manage your negative feelings of frustration and anger and prevents us from acting out our negative emotions. The adult ego state is non- threatening.

It is the part of the self that analyses and solves problems. It is assumed to be fully developed by the time we reach the age of twelve.

I shall be clean

An adult ego state contains statements that are exploratory rather than judgemental, solution focused in an emotionally neutrol tone that promotes non defensiveness.

Once we become aware of our ego-states we can move ourselves out of and into which ever one we need for the here and now situation.

When communicating with your dealer the following diagram is the unhealthy position to be in!

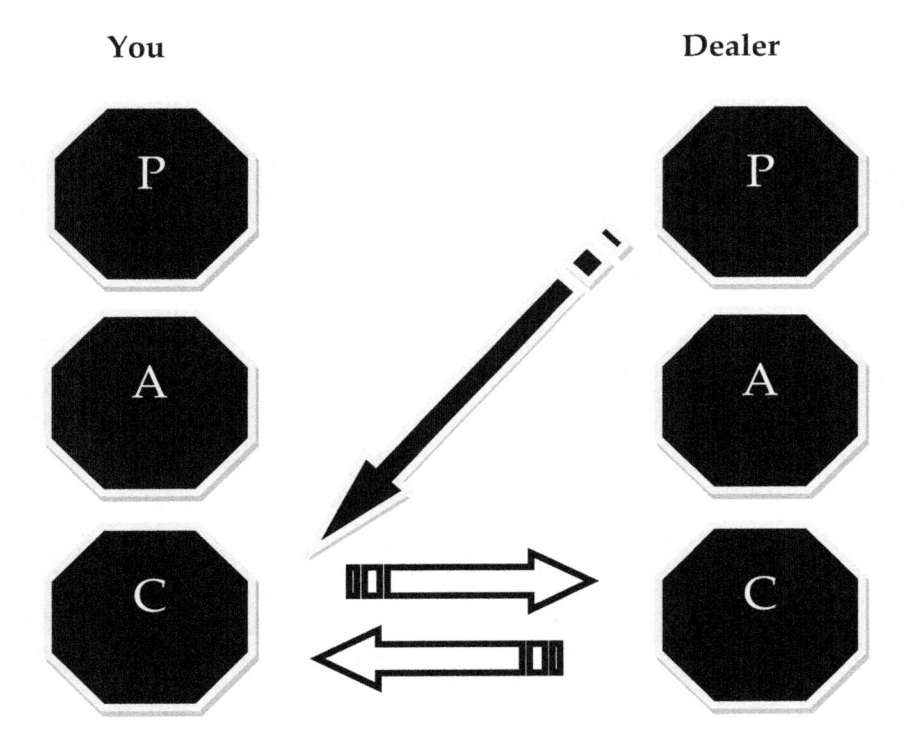

You   **Dealer**

P   P

A   A

C   C

BLACK ARROW - This is the position where the Dealer is hooking into your Child from his or her Parent ego state. An example of that is:

Dealer: "I have some fantastic gear; I can give it to you for half the street cost" **(Parent ego state)**

I shall be clean

You: "Oh thanks, uhm that's great. How much is it?" **(child ego state)**

Dealer: "Don't tell anyone else but you can have it for a tenner" **(child ego state)**

It is the position when your Dealer is condescending towards you. His Parent ego state is talking to your Child ego state. It makes sense that this is not going to instigate a transaction that is helpful for you.

WHITE ARROWS - The other interaction (the arrows are both pointing in the direction of each other's child ego state) is when both of you are in child ego state, and communicating on a childish level.

An example of that is:

Dealer: "Hey buster, bet you can't guess what I have got?" **(child ego state)**

You: "So, what?"

Dealer: "It's the best gear on the market, but you wont be able to afford it. Nah Nah Nah Nah **(child ego state)**

You: "I'll have some now, what you got?" (Proving a point) **(child ego state)**

The dealer has hooked your child straight away, just as he mean's to.

Be aware that a dealer will try to hook your child ego state from both his/her parent ego state or his/her own child ego state.

The idea is <u>NOT TO LET HIM!</u>

In this instance he did, and you have the choice to stay in child ego state or move to a different state. To help you shift into adult ego state think about your body posture, if your shoulders are slumped then this puts you in child ego state immediately. Others pick up on this especially dealers.

This can happen in many situations, for example your boss tells you he wants you to come to his office at three pm. Straight away

I shall be clean

you will more than likely go into your child ego state and worry about what you have done wrong.

For a few hours you will have anxiety, even feel like going home. But if you can shift yourself back into adult ego state, you will reality test and say to yourself. It might not be anything I have done wrong; it might actually be to tell me I have a pay rise.

Even if you have done something 'wrong' staying in adult helps you to manage this a bitter better and stop your boss from hooking your child.

Now let's look at this change we talked about, the secret weapon of change, the weapon that will stop the dealer from hooking into your inner child, and manipulating you into taking drugs.

The following diagram is the healthy position to be in when interacting with your dealers:

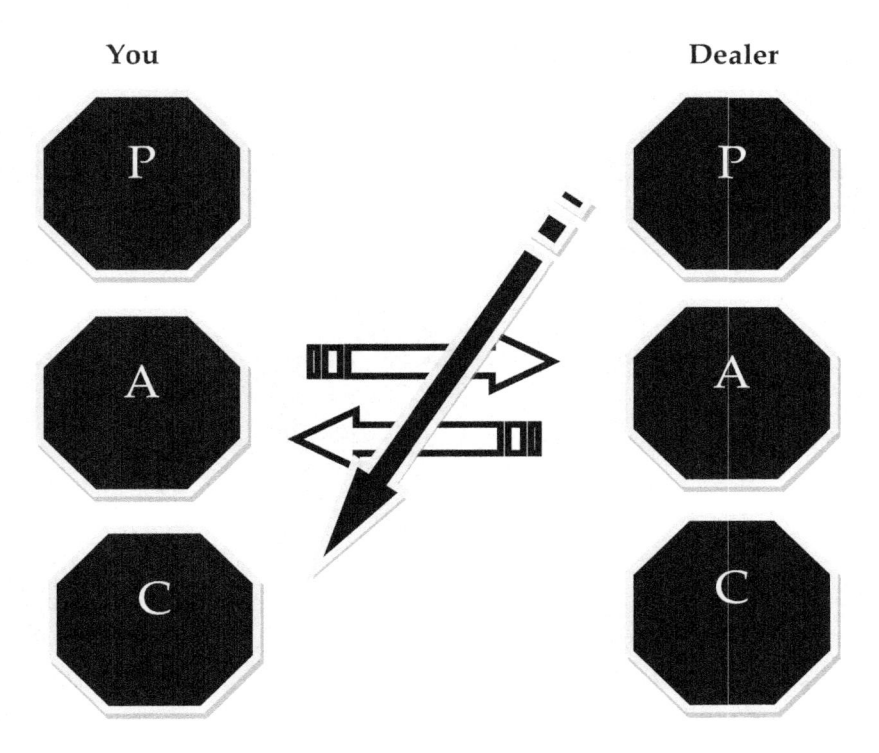

You   **Dealer**

P   P

A   ⇄   A

C   C

I shall be clean

Let's use the above examples again only this time interacting from one of the above positions:

Dealer: I have some fantastic gear; I can give it to you for half the street cost" **(Parent ego state)**

You: "Oh thank you, but not today" **(Adult ego state)**

Dealer: "Oh okay see you later" **(Adult ego state)**

And

Dealer: "Hey buster, bet you can't guess what I have got?" **(child ego state)**

You: "No, buts if it's drugs not for me thanks"**(Adult ego state)**

Dealer: "Oh okay" **(Adult ego state)**

Can you see the difference in interactions?

The idea is not to let anyone hook into the 'child' part of you that is vulnerable, and may lead you to react in a way that is not going to get you the respect that you need.

If you 'lose it' with your then the other person has hooked into your own child ego state.

Be mindful when your parents are getting on at you for your drug use, they are in their child ego state because they are scared. Communicate back from your adult. If you stay in adult other people may shift into their adult too.

Mum in her child ego state

This takes some practice and you may, especially when tired, ill, or menopausal, fall back into old pattern. If this happens then that is okay you just make the switch there and then and start again.

I shall be clean

Just one other point I need to reiterate is that to be in any of these ego states is healthy when you are in them at the right time.

I shall be clean

CHAPTER EIGHT
Early Experiences

We all have early experiences that have been painful for us and due to this we develop behaviours to mask the pain or to protect us from re-experiencing this pain. One of those behaviours may be drug use.

What amazes me when I learn about clients lives and we do a lifeline together is the link between their drug use and their painful experiences.

Ninety nine percent of the time we would learn together that they started their drug use after a painful experience and their drug use changed each time they experienced similar painful experiences.

They would go on a different or harder drug or change the way they used that drug i.e moved from smoking to injecting.

TIME LINE EXAMPLE:

AGE	EXPERIENCES	DRUG USE
0 - 7	Moved house due to Dads job, so had to move schools as well leaving behind my friends.	
7-11	Mum and Dad split up so we moved back to where we had lived up until I was seven. I had to go back to my old school which was embarrassing. Dad stopped seeing us when I	Age 12 starting sniffing gas

I shall be clean

	was 9 as he met someone else and said he was going to start a new life. Mum met someone else who was nice but he went to prison.	
11 - 16	Moved house again to a different area, had to leave friends and school again. Was doing well at school but new school was much further ahead so I lost interest and messed about. Mum's parenting was inconsistent. I was good at electrics and mending things, so she would treat me like a man to look after my sisters and mend things but then say I had to be in at 8 o'clock at night	Age 13 started smoking cannabis
16 - 21	Mum rejected me because of my drug use, she was always grounding me so I went to live with my paternal grandparents. They let me do what I liked so my drug use increased. Had my first serious relationship and she fell pregnant we had a baby girl when I was 17 I was happy then but we split up when I was about 18/19. We fought all the time it was a volatile relationship. Just went from relationship to relationship then and job to job.	Age 16 started using stimulants as well as cannabis
21 - 30	I wasn't allowed to see my	Started

I shall be clean

	daughter. Another girl I was with fell pregnant, we split up when she was pregnant so I never saw this baby either. Met another girl this relationship was very dramatic and I never knew where I stood with her. Most girls I have been out with I have felt very insecure. My life was very chaotic didn't see my mum or my sisters.	smoking heroin Started injecting heroin

Can you see a theme running through this person's life. He has experienced a lot of rejection and loss. My guess is that each time he experiences rejection or loss then this would be a trigger to use and a change in his drug using behaviour.

Working in this way would be exploring a client's core material, so healthy coping mechanisms need to be in place first otherwise the drug use could increase, particularly if their history is a painful one.

Each time the person above experienced their psychological wound or sometimes known as early wound it would have been overwhelmingly painful.

To give you a sense of this have you ever picked the scar from a wound before it has healed? Or have you heard the saying "Pouring salt on an old wound?" Imagine how painful this would be. This is what we experience when someone picks at or pours salt on an old psychological or emotional wound that has never been healed.

I shall be clean

Once you have been wounded, or perceived to have been wounded then to re-experience a similar incident is like putting salt on an already existing wound.

That is because when we develop a wound we become sensitive to factors that would not usually bother us. This is why different things affect different people in different ways. We all have different wounds, depending on our own personal experiences.

This is also why it is sometimes difficult to understand why some people are upset over things that others would not generally get upset about; chances are that it is because it has penetrated an already open wound.

Why do some people feel bad when someone promises to call and does not and yet for others it is no real issue?

Why do you think some people hate the feeling of being out of control, and yet others are far more laid back? Why do some people deal with rejection much better than others? Why are some people more able to confront abuse than others? It is because rejection, abandonment, being out of control, abuse is not their wound.

If we suffer painfully when experiencing for example rejection or abandonment it could be because people who did not approve of us rejected us in the past, and so whenever someone ignores us in the present it hurts like hell. Not because it should hurt, but because it touched an old wound and reminded us of a past hurt.

Applying for a job and getting a rejection letter for example, would upset most people, but people with a fear of 'rejection' would be devastated and feel broken.

It is because we all have different 'crumple buttons,' different wounds.

If you try to just escape or forget about these wounds, they don't go away, they will come back to remind you that they are there each time you feel rejected or hurt or abused or even engulfed.

These wounds make you vulnerable! Things that do not bother some people can prevent others from sleeping at night, because they are wounds that haven't healed.

Before we can heal any of these wounds we should first

I shall be clean

identify what they are, where they came from and know the reason behind the wound. When you know the root cause, healing the wound is the easy part.

If you block out these wounds or ignore them, they never leave you alone; you will continue to revisit the pain time after time, each time you feel the negative feeling that is your early wound.

Psychodynamic therapy which is often more long term therapy helps you to heal those wounds and part of the process is to revisit those early experiences and re experience the pain. This is usually done well into the therapy to enable the relationship to develop between you and your therapist and to enable you both to see what these wounds are by talking and exploration.

It can be a painful process but from my own personal experience, once you have done this, when a familiar situation arises again in your life, although it can be hurtful, it is nothing like the overwhelming emotion that you once felt and much easier to deal with. It is not until then that you realise that the healing has happened the wound has healed. You will find yourself dealing with the situation in a very different way.

Once you have identified your wounds, and have recognized their origin, then the healing can begin.

Identifying your pain is about allowing yourself to 'feel it,' staying with the pain. Often when we feel an uncomfortable, negative feeling we do our utmost to avoid it, we do this by keeping busy, using substances such as drugs or alcohol, gambling, going for a walk, going to the gym, reading a book, sexual activity etc.

Although these are coping strategies that may work for you, they are quick fixes. The pain does not go away, it will return when you least expect it and bite you on the bum. It will be a double whammy, because you have not yet healed the original wound.

What is the worst that can happen to you if you stay with the pain? You won't die. It won't send you mad. It will be extremely uncomfortable and you may cry for England. But crying is healthy; it is a release of all the emotion to allow you to then think more clearly.

I shall be clean

Emotional growth is a life long journey, just as you work through one part of 'self,' something else may come along and the work begins again, but each time you do this you will feel better and function in a more healthy way. The first time is the hardest because you don't know what to expect, after this you will find it easier to work on all your emotional wounds as they arise.

Being lost is part of life's process, staying lost will cause you more emotional turmoil.

Find a safe place at a safe time. Sit or lay comfortably. Put your hand on your stomach or wherever you feel the emotional pain and ask yourself:

> **What am I feeling?**
> **When have I felt like this before?**
> **How many times do I feel like this?**
> **What is the theme running through these experiences?**

This will help you to discover your wound and help you to take the first step towards healing.

Imagine someone cut you with a knife on your arm and before this had chance to heal, someone else cut you in the same place. Can you imagine how much this would hurt? Then someone cut you again and again in this same place. What would you imagine you would do?

My guess is that you would develop strategies to protect yourself from being cut in that same place again. Maybe you would buy a thick jacket or wear a plaster cast. Or you might avoid going out of the house or shout at people to keep them at a distance.

We do exactly the same thing with psychological or emotional wounds, although these wounds are usually invisible and much harder to describe, and are not always in our conscious awareness.

When we have experienced something painful and we re-experience that same pain, we develop strategies, behaviours to protect ourselves

Exploring your psychological wound can be painful. I would

I shall be clean

recommend that if your early life experiences were particularly traumatic that you do this work in a safe environment with a reputable therapist.

There are five primary wounds that a therapist might look at with you. These are:

Abuse
Abandonment
Rejection
Engulfment
Neglect

There are needless to say, various degrees of these wounds. Abandonment for example: There are mild to severe forms of abandonment. Mild would be someone who got lost out shopping with mum, to someone who has been adopted and experiences feelings of abandonment, to someone whose parents left them at home and never returned. The same applies to all of the wounds.

If your wound is severe in nature then again I would strongly advise that you do this work which could be extremely painful with a therapist.

It is also important to remember that our wounds could be perceived experiences.

Even if you do not access therapy to work on any early wounds, at least you have an insight in what experiences may trigger you to use.

Maybe you could sit and do your own lifeline with a therapist or your key worker if you are in treatment, and look to see if there are any themes running through your life. To help you to recognize any early experiences that resurrect old pain that may trigger your use. You could then use the strategies from chapter four to chapter six to manage these in a healthier way.

Once you know your wound you can plan strategies to manage

I shall be clean

the pain. They strategies you use already I would guess sets you up for what you most fear. Let's look at this example:

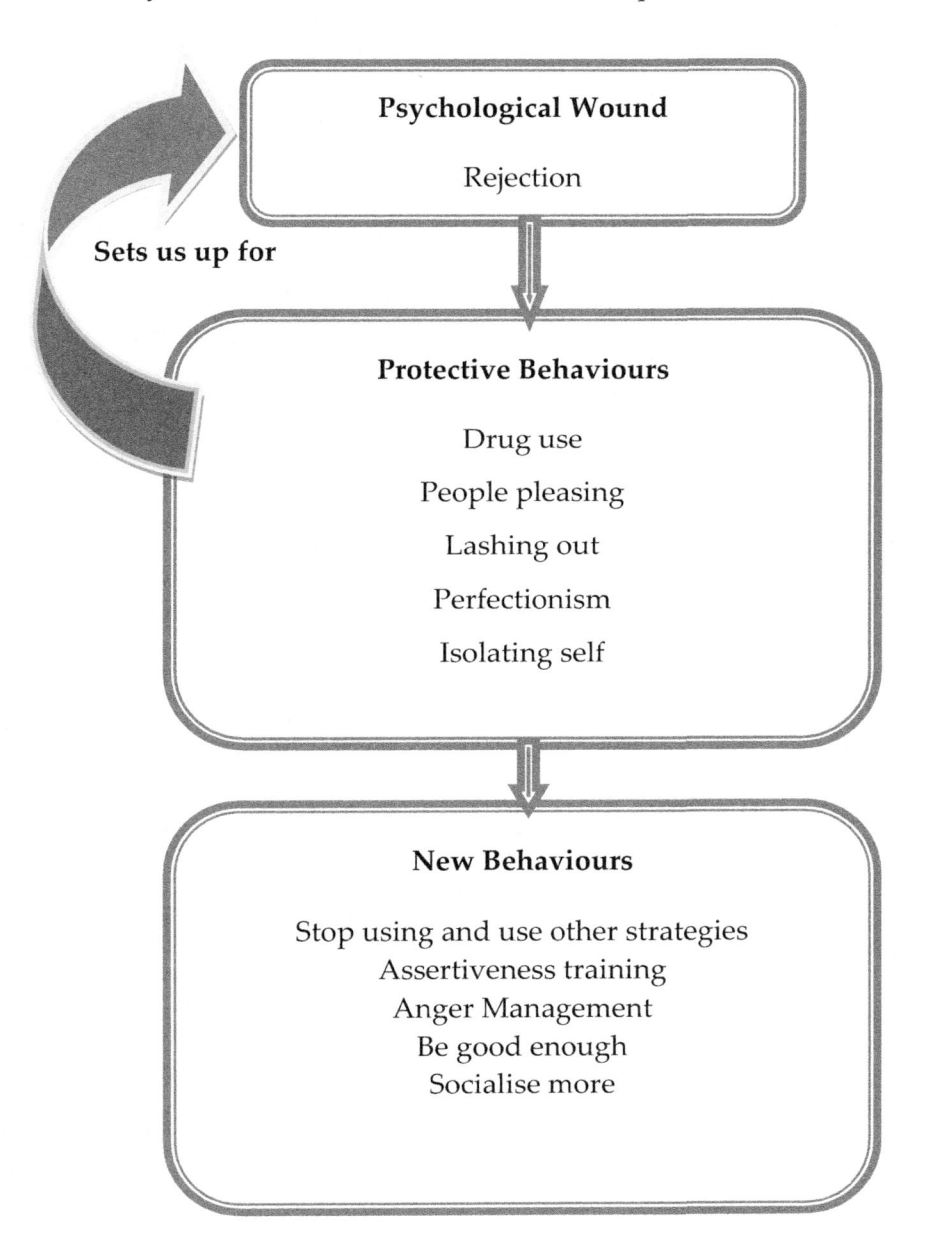

Psychological Wound

Rejection

Sets us up for

Protective Behaviours

Drug use
People pleasing
Lashing out
Perfectionism
Isolating self

New Behaviours

Stop using and use other strategies
Assertiveness training
Anger Management
Be good enough
Socialise more

I shall be clean

As you will see from this example, the behaviours that we develop to protect ourselves from being, in this example 'rejection' only serve to set us up for further 'rejection'. They may have worked once but they don't work anymore. So as you can see we have to develop new behaviours, healthier ones.

Have a go at this with your therapist or support worker.

The important thing to understand is that we do not be too hard on ourselves for developing these protective behaviours, they were there for a reason and they were developed because we had not been taught any alternative emotional regulation tools.

"When the past calls, let it go to voicemail. Believe me, it has nothing new to say."

I shall be clean

CHAPTER NINE
Ambivalence & Sabotage

Ambivalence is a normal aspect of human nature; passing through ambivalence is a natural phase in the process of change.

It is when you get *stuck* in ambivalence that problems can persist and build up.

Ambivalence is a reasonable place to visit, but you wouldn't want to live there!

"I WANT TO AND I DON'T WANT TO"

To explore ambivalence is to work at the heart of the problem of being stuck. Until you can resolve the "I want to, but I don't want to" dilemma, change is likely to be slow-going and short lived.

The question to ask yourself is not "Why aren't you motivated?" but rather "what are you motivated to do at this present time.

Let's look at this together:

Exercise Eleven

Write down a list of what you are willing to do at this time:

Example:

I shall be clean

I am willing to:
Explore my drug use
Make a reduction plan
When I feel angry try some anger management rather than use

Now write down a list of what you are not willing to do:

I am not willing to:
Stop my drug use altogether
Stop using when I go clubbing

Well thats a good start you have already begun to explore your ambivalence. Well done. You may not see your drug use as a problem yet and want to continue without making any changes.

You may be in two minds thinking about change. You may have acknowledged that there are one or more things about continuing your drug use that are a problem or are no longer good for you. BUT you still enjoy it.

You may have made a decision to change, and are preparing to change but have not done so yet. You may have put the idea of change into practice and may have very recently given up or cut down. You may have kept up your change in use over time and in the process of reaching your goals. You may have given up, however lapsed and resumed using substances either a little or a lot.

You may be thinking of therapy to work through some of the 'stuff' you can't work through on your own, or you may be still working on some of your strategies in this book and learning new triggers, along the way.

These are all stages of change that you may be at, and are the normal processes of change.

Or indeed you may have made a decision that now is not the right time for you to change or stop your drug use.

This is okay. One day you will make a decision to stop using, you may make the choice never to stop. To help you to explore if this is

I shall be clean

the right choice for you. Try this:

Exercise Twelve

What I would like you to do now is I would like you to follow these directions to explore your future:

1. Look at the floor in the room where you are now sitting and draw an imaginary line at the furthest wall.
2. Where you are sitting or standing now is the age you are now. The end of the line is the end of your life. Let's imagine that is 90 years old.
3. I would like you to walk to where you think on your line would be you 20 years older.
4. Now close your eyes
5. You are twenty years older and still using drugs
6. What are you thinking?
7. What are you feeling?
8. What is life like for you right now?
9. What are you doing?
10. What is it like living in your world right now?
11. Use all your senses, smell, taste, sight and ears and really feel your life in 20 years time as a drug user.
12. Open your eyes and move back
13. Now close them again and move back to twenty years older again.
14. You are 20 years older and you gave up drugs 20 years ago
15. What are you thinking?
16. What are you feeling?
17. What is life like for you right now?
18. What are you doing?
19. What is it like living in your world right now>

I shall be clean

20. **Use all your senses, smell, taste, sight and ears and really feel your life in 20 years time as a non drug user.**
21. **Open your eyes**
22. **Now go back to your original place, where you are now, the age you are now.**

What did that exercise tell you? Did it tell you that you are ready to change?

Games we play and responsibility:

Some of your ambivalence might be because you are playing what I call the 'blame game' or 'Plom' – poor little old me. That might sound harsh but as human beings we can all play psychological games at times in our life.

Games are ways of getting what we want without facing up to our underlying motives. They are always dishonest and often manipulative.

Some of the purposes of games are:

To gain love, attention and reassurance.
To get what we want without saying it directly – especially when what we want is not considered acceptable.
To be right, without blame, even when we are not.
To avoid facing the truth.
To free ourselves of guilt or responsibility.
To be aggressive without guilt or facing the consequences.
To reinforce our own bad feelings about ourselves or unrealistically good feelings about ourselves.

Substance misuse problems are often related to having certain problems in life. Your drug using behaviour may have increased following problems in your family, the breakdown of a relationship or losing your job.

In some cases as described in chapter seven it may be a way of

I shall be clean

blocking out unpleasant or disturbing memories, maybe from your childhood.

When you have experienced difficult times, it is natural to want to blame others for your problems. It is very tempting to say "I'm using because my wife left me...", or "because I'm angry with my mum"

The fact is, though, that your drug use is your problem – not theirs. This is because you chose to use drugs to manage these things. In other words it might not be your fault what has happened to you, but it was your choice in how you manage the pain, the thoughts, and the situation. You could have made different choices.

You are the only person who can put things right. One of the main keys to overcoming a drug problem is to accept that *you* are responsible for the way in which you choose to manage difficult times and more importantly you are responsible for your recovery.

Yes you may have gone through a pretty tough time and people may have given you a hard time but it was your choice to manage that by taking drugs. Therefore you cannot blame others for the choice you made in managing these difficult times.

We manage things better when we can take 'responsibility' for example if you ended up in a relationship that was destructive/bad it helps if we say to ourselves 'that relationship was not good for me, it was destructive but I chose at the time to enter into that relationship, believing that it would be good.'

Obviously, with abuse, sexual assault we cannot take responsibility, but the choice we can make is that we are not going to give this person the power to destroy the rest of our lives, we can have therapy and learn how to manage the emotions from this dreadful experience in a different way, a healthy way we can choose to heal the wound that had been caused to us.

Your family and friends can give you tremendous support but they cannot do it for you. Your key/drug worker can also help but it is you that is going to have to cope when times get tough. You have to accept that you are the main person who can make the necessary changes in your life. Do this and you will have more than a fighting

I shall be clean

chance of overcoming your addiction.

BURIDIAN'S ASS

This is the story of a donkey that stands alone in a field; either side of him is a stack of hay.

He can't decide which to eat first – so he stands there……...................

Undecided.

Night turns into day and he stands there…………………….

Still undecided.

Until he starves to death!

EVEN DOING NOTHING IS A CHOICE, YOU MAKE THE CHOICE TO DO NOTHING OR YOU MAKE THE CHOICE TO DO SOMETHING. BOTH ARE A CHOICE.

I shall be clean

Exercise Thirteen

Are you wearing a watch or a ring at the moment? If not can you imagine that you are. Okay I want you to put your watch or ring on the other arm/finger.

What does that feel like?

You will probably say things like:

> Weird, uncomfortable, strange, difficult

That is what change is like

Now I would like you to imagine that I asked you to keep it on that arm/finger for a week.

I again ask you, what does that feel like now?

You will probably say something like:

I forgot it was there, normal, comfortable, it would probably feel strange going back to the other arm /finger now.

That is what change is like

Change feels uncomfortable at first, it will feel strange but eventually it will feel normal and comfortable and you will feel healthier and more balanced both physically and psychologically.

I shall be clean

Changing your substance misuse will feel like that at first, but after a short while it will feel normal to be 'drug free', it will feel more comfortable.

Growth is painful. Change is painful. But nothing is as painful as staying stuck somewhere you don't belong. Your life will not getter better by chance, it will get better by change.

Stop being afraid of what could go wrong and start to become excited about what could go right. Many clients say to me when discussing change "what if I land in a lorry load of sh.t?" – My response to them is "what if you land in a lorry load of roses? Until you start to make changes you will never know, but what you can do is steer clear of the crap and head for the roses.

Sabotage

Now I would like to talk about sabotage, which is a very common behaviour of drug users, they may sabotage treatment and often they do not understand why.

If this is you then it is important that you explore this as if you don't then it is likely that the same thing will happen over and over again in your treatment and as I said earlier the more you fail at abstinence the harder it becomes to believe that you can do it.

I have met many clients who sabotage treatment, get clean and

I shall be clean

then a couple of weeks or months later they are back in treatment again and they do this for different reasons. I will give you two case samples:

Case Studies

Fred (pseudo name) had been in for a detoxification off heroin about five times. Each time he had remained clean for about two months. He wanted to have a detoxification again, however his key worker referred him to me to explore with him what had gone wrong on his previous attempts.

I explored this with him and what we learned is that when he was using all his family were around every day, paying him attention, doing things for him, helping him, doing his meals because they knew he wouldn't, helping him to pay his bills, giving him lots of affection.

However when he had recovered and left hospital and was abstinent, he didn't see them as much. They left him to his own devises, to sort his own life out.

For this client he sabotaged to get his own needs met. It would have been more helpful if his family had done things the other way around. However I could see what was happening, whilst he was using drugs they were worried about him and so became very hands on in trying to help him, but once he had stopped using drugs they could get on with their own lives, felt that they did not have to run around after him anymore.

For Fred though he became lonely during these times, he felt that no-one cared. He missed the attention. Negative attention is

I shall be clean

better than no attention so he would sabotage his treatment just to feel cared for again. This was all on an unconscious level.

Once this came into his awareness Fred was able to see this and communicate this to his family it made his sixth attempt at recovery a successful one.

> Freda's children had been taken into care because of her chaotic drug using behaviour. She was devastated and determined to stop using to get her children back.
>
> She succeeded however getting her children back was not as easy as she believed it would be. Social services needed to see her maintain this abstinence. She began using drugs again.

We explored this and learned that she was using to manage the pain of losing her children and also wanted social services to see how painful it was for her. "See because you would not give me my children back, I am back on drugs" – The 'blame game' as discussed earlier in this chapter. Social services were not responsible for how Freda managed her pain.

For Freda she had sabotaged treatment in an attempt to make social services understand her pain and give her the children back. Needless to say it did not work; in fact it worked against her rather than for her.

Once she was able to see this, that stamping her feet, was not a 'behaviour' that was going to get her needs met she was able to stop again, work on healthier emotional regulation tools and work with social services and prove that she could maintain her abstinence.

I shall be clean

She eventually got her children back.

Exercise Fourteen

Does this sound like you? Do you stop and then sabotage your recovery? If so try to explore this by asking yourself the following questions:

> What are the advantages to my use?
> What needs do I hope to get met by continuing my use?
> What needs do I get met by continuing my use?
> What are the disadvantages when I stop?
> What needs are no longer met?
> Do I like playing the 'blame game'?
> Does it punish someone else in my life when I use?
> Who is the one that is suffering the most from my sabotaging behaviour?

Once you have done this it might be worth looking at other ways of getting your needs met, maybe you might need to communicate with your family to get their support in your recovery. Or maybe you need to reality test who is really getting punished when you play out these behaviours.

WELL DONE YOU HAVE BEEN ABLE TO EXPLORE MORE OF YOUR DRUG USING BEHAVIOUR.

I shall be clean

"Everyone has inside of him a piece of good news. The good news is that you don't know how great you can be! How much you can love! What you can accomplish! And what your potential is!"

I shall be clean

CHAPTER TEN
Parenting

A lot of people feel that using drugs does not impact on their children's lives. It does though in many ways.
Children are naturally curious creatures and like to watch their parents and emulate them. Think of the children who dress up in mummy or daddy's clothes. Copy mum with her make up or dad with his DIY. This is the way children learn and I have seen many a child with a lolly stick (or something similar) in their mouths pretending to smoke a cigarette.

Drug users have said to me over the years "they don't understand what I am doing when I am rolling a joint or preparing my fix, they are far too young." I say you're right they don't now but they sure will when they are older, and you have just normalised it for them, so it is inevitable that your child will become a drug user, believing it to be ok.

Think about a child that walks into Mum and Dad's bedroom in the middle of the night and they are making love. That child doesn't know what mummy and daddy are doing, but he doesn't forget it and he sure understands what they were doing once he reaches fourteen.

I shall be clean

This is the same with drugs, he may not know at six but he will remember it and know what you were doing once he's a teenager. He may even lack respect for you and that is the last thing you want when he is going through the terrible teens.

Also you are teaching your children how to regulate their emotions, which will be naturally overwhelming when they are teenagers. Ask yourself this when they are 'flooding' in normal teenager feelings, are you going to sit them down and say "Here honey have a fix, that will make you feel better?" I have not met a drug user yet, that answers 'yes' to that question. They look at me horrified.

Using drugs affects different parents in different ways. But children of drug users are more likely to be neglected than other children, and are more likely to use drugs themselves.

Parents who use drugs or alcohol do not necessarily do a bad job of caring for their children. But problem use of drugs or alcohol can lead to detrimental effects on child growth and development.

Children raised in homes where parents are regularly taking drugs are more likely to have problems with brain development and learning, and difficulties with emotional control, behaviour and social adjustment.

Children of substance-abusing parents are at greater risk of child abuse and neglect, and are less likely to be well looked after.

Children whose parents use drugs are more likely to use drugs when they grow up – usually the same drugs that their parents use.

So you may be creating a generational cycle of drug use. Ask yourself this:

Do you really want your kids to grow up using drugs?

Do you really want them to experience the same problems that you are experiencing?

I shall be clean

No parent has ever said to me "I don't mind if my kids use drugs when they are older." All of them have said that they would prefer their kids not to use. How is that going to be manageable if you are normalising it for them?

Using drugs doesn't make someone a bad parent. Many parents use drugs such as alcohol in a low-risk way. Other parents use drugs more heavily and cope remarkably well, doing the best that they can in difficult circumstances.

But **using drugs can negatively affect your ability to parent**. In some cases, it can also directly affect your child. When parental drug use harms the child in some way, it becomes a problem.

Sometimes when parents take drugs, the effects can have lasting impacts on the child's development and behaviour.

For example, drug-using parents might:

Drive when intoxicated and with the children in the car

Forget about care the children need, such as getting meals or getting children to school

Let children see distressing mood swings or behaviour.

Not be as involved in children's daily lives as they ordinarily would be this might mean missing important events, like school concerts and parties.

Forgetting to get their P.E. Kit ready and a child having to make excuses can be embarrassing for them, particularly if they have to wear one out the 'spares' box, two sizes too big for them.

Being too stoned to read them a bedtime story, may seem something little to you but can be distressing for them

I shall be clean

Children may feel uncomfortable about having friends over, which can make it harder for the children to learn social skills.

And that is just to name but a few

Think of all the things that you have not been able to do for your children due to your substance misuse?

There are times in all parents' lives when we cannot be totally emotionally there for our children, i.e. when under stress, having suffered a loss or relationship breakdown.

Parents **cannot** be totally emotionally there for their children when under the influence of drugs or alcohol. Children who grow up with very little emotional support from their parents have numerous problems of their own as adults, i.e. difficulty expressing their emotions, difficulty in forming relationships, difficulty in supporting their own children's emotional needs, and difficulty in getting their own needs met because they have grown up believing that their needs are unimportant.

Smoking parents might expose their children to second-hand smoke. Studies have linked parental smoking – even when the children are nowhere near the smoke.

Some people use drugs and alcohol in social situations to have a good time or to relax and unwind. Other people use drugs to deal with unhappiness and problems with self-esteem, or to cover up feelings of guilt or shame. Some live in circumstances where drugs are part of their immediate culture, such as in areas of poverty where drug misuse is higher or in parts of the country that embrace 'alternative' culture.

Taking drugs can affect the way you do things and the way you think.

Some people feel that drugs have positive effects. But drugs can also have serious negative effects on your health and relationships.

Depending on the drug, the amount used and the context of use, drugs can make you:

I shall be clean

> **Become anxious and upset**
> **Lose coordination**
> **Become aggressive or forgetful**
> **Lose awareness of what is happening around you.**

Because drugs can also affect your ability to react and your accuracy in doing things, it is much easier to have an accident when you are doing things such as driving a car or even cooking over a hot stove.

It is important to have all your reactions alert when looking after children to prevent them from accidents and dangers of their own.

Using drugs during pregnancy can be harmful for the baby. They can be born with withdrawal symptoms which can be distressing to see. Coming into the world is traumatic enough for a new born baby without feeling extremely ill when s/he gets here.

Wouldn't it be nice to bring our children into a drug free world?

Allowing them to be children and not have to worry about their parents drug use.

Children do worry about their parents; they worry about losing them and when they hear at school how dangerous drugs are this can cause them distress that they may hide from you. This then may come out in behavioural problems because this is often how children express their feelings.

This chapter is by no means meant to criticize you as a drug using parent. It is to hopefully bring you to awareness of the effects that your substance misuse may have on your children.

Many drug using parents that I have worked with were not aware and when I gave them this information they were surprised and it often gave them the motivation to make changes.

I hope that it does the same for you.

I shall be clean

CHAPTER ELEVEN
Stopping & Relapse Prevention

If you have decided to stop using altogether then you will need to work out a plan on how to do this.

This might mean a visit to your local substance misuse service, the staff there are usually very qualified and are used to working with people like you. The staff will have empathy for your situation and are non judgemental and experienced in the substance misuse field. They will meet with you and collect as much information as possible from you so that together you can develop a care plan.

Treatment options will be discussed with you at either your first or second visit. If it is felt that you have a physical dependency, usually for people who are using heroin then your treatment may involve a detoxification or substitute medication programme. This is because you may experience physical withdrawals when you try to stop.

For most other drugs they will offer you support in reducing or abstaining often using some of the skills mentioned in this book.

When you begin this process you may experience cravings. So here are some tips on how to manage cravings:

Cravings:

Everyone experiences the uncomfortable craving or urge to use drugs. After all you have been using for some time and it is inevitable that you will miss using drugs at first.

I shall be clean

It is important to know that cravings or urges to use, although not very pleasant are only thoughts and feelings and cannot hurt you. They will only last for a period of time and YOU CAN push through it if you believe you can.

Some people think of cravings as a wave that builds up, peaks and crashes over them and is then over.

You are a surfer surfing your urge or craving to use. Imagine the craving as a wave next time it happens. Time it if you like and notice how it builds up and fades away.

Think of the 3 Ds when experiencing cravings:

Delay: Cravings only last for a period of time and will pass – so delay using or drinking for a minute at a time until it passes.

Distract: Do some other activity that matches with the energy of your craving to distract yourself – brisk exercise or dig the garden.

Decide: Make that decision not to use – think of all the things that you don't like about using. All the things you have to lose. Cravings only remind you of the good things about using so challenge those thoughts and remember all the reasons why you have decided to change in the first place.

Look back at the lists you have made throughout this book to help remind you.

Cravings will be one of the biggest areas that you will have to deal with when coming off substances.

There are four main areas of craving associated with any form of misuse and you need to understand where they come from, how they work, what preceded them and more importantly, how to avoid/stop them.

I shall be clean

There are two golden rules to remember:

They always need a trigger (face, place etc)
They are not a need, they are a want

Cravings can be a combination of physical and emotional factors.

The physical factors may be:

Sweating, heart is beating faster, butterflies in stomach, anxiety and increased breathing rate come from the release of adrenaline into the system triggering off a <u>fight or flight</u> response.

The Emotional Factors may be:

Depression, boredom, isolation, anger, anxiety, pain etc

There are four types of cravings to look out for:

Craving when first stopping: These are usually triggered by the initial 'crash' or 'come down'. The down experienced, when you have felt so high, makes you want to use more even when you know that the 'buzz' felt is not going to be as high as the last one.

Conscious craving: You are aware of what is happening and what you want. This type of craving may fit into your pattern of use such as time of day, day of week, faces and places. You know the cause so you have a choice.

Unconscious craving: More complicated, more prevalent when you are trying to give up. A complicated string of events may build up to

I shall be clean

get you into the using position. Justifications will be in place and you will start to bullshit yourself.

Unexpected craving: This happens further down the line of recovery. You have been clean for some time and you begin to feel confident. An event happens that you don't feel so confident about – child's first day at school or college, or something that generates actual real fear – dentist, doctors, and threats to yourself etc. These events will trigger off a genuine release of adrenaline. Couple this with an emotional uncertainty and the need for the 'hit' will be strong.

If you have done the exercises in this book you will be very aware of your triggers to using and the situations, places that may be a risk to relapse.

When experiencing these situations without drugs you may feel uncomfortable and unsure of how to cope. You may experience cravings, so it is very important to have an action plan in place.

Therefore you may want to revisit the work that you did around triggers and the strategies that you put together to avoid or manage these situation.

In these situations it's vital that you have good support. If you have to attend somewhere that may trigger your drug use, for example, take a friend who knows about your problems and can give you encouragement.

Try doing one or all of the following:

Telling all your friends that you are clean and sober.

Throw out all your drugs and drug paraphernalia

Throwing out telephone numbers for your dealers/change your phone number

I shall be clean

Cancel your credit card/cash card, have someone hold your money

If you have any money and you are tempted to use, carry a stamped addressed envelope around with you and if you are tempted put any money you have in the envelope and pop it in the post box by the time you get it the craving will have gone.

Take a different route home to avoid passing places associated with your drug use

Redecorating or re-arrange the room in which drugs were used

It is also helpful to rehearse some answers you can use if you're being pressured to take drugs.

These could include:

"I can't I'm on medication at the moment"
"I've got to drive home later".
"I'm having a break at the moment from drugs"
"No thanks I'm feeling a little under the weather"
"No thanks I have to be somewhere tomorrow so I need my wits about me"

Or be brave and say

"No thanks I've given up"

Write some of your own ideas in your journal.
You should gradually develop an effective range of strategies and techniques. In time the association of drugs with your triggers

I shall be clean

will diminish and they will be less and less difficult.

One of the most difficult things that I experience substance users to have difficulty with when trying to stop and is a high risk to relapse is sleep. They find it difficult to sleep.

I hope that these tips can support you with this:

If you are reducing, or have recently stopped using then your sleep pattern will also be disturbed. Try to be patient this will improve with time, try be gentle with yourself and don't push yourself to hard, as this can lead to frustration and even lapses.

Nightmares are common when withdrawing from substances and usually stop after a short period of time. If they do occur, try to be rational and don't panic. The reason for this is that there are three stages to sleep:

> Stage One: is where we are just dropping off however could wake up at the slightest sound. It is where we are drifting in and out of sleep.
>
> Stage Two: is where we have fallen into our sleep, and are sleeping soundly.
>
> Stage Three: in where we are in a very deep sleep and this is when dreams occur

When we use drugs and alcohol we very rarely reach the Stage Three level of sleep. If you think back to your drug using days you will probably observe that you didn't have many, if any dreams then.

Once you have stopped using, those dreams will come like a flood. Sigmund Freud a well known psychiatrist said that our dreams are our unconscious thoughts and feelings coming to the surface. Well if you think about it, while you have been using substances you have been suppressing all those thoughts and

I shall be clean

feelings. Therefore it is inevitable that they are going to come pouring out now, just like they may do in your waking hours too.

But like any flood, it will stop eventually. It would be a good idea to try to start making a routine for yourself to help you to sleep.

Try eating a small meal in the evening, nothing too heavy as this may cause indigestion.

Keep a regular schedule. Try to go to bed and wake up at the same time every day, even on the weekends. Keeping a regular schedule will help your body expect sleep at the same time each day. Don't oversleep to make up for sleep lost. This will only disrupt your sleep pattern and try not to nap in the day.

Reduce stimulant intake. Substances such as cocaine, ecstasy and amphetamine are going to have serious impact on sleep. Also legal stimulants like pro-plus will prevent you sleeping

Limit caffeine and alcohol. Avoid drinking caffeinated or alcoholic beverages such as tea, coffee, coke and red bull for several hours before bedtime. Although alcohol may initially act as a sedative, it can interrupt normal sleep patterns and produces poor quality sleep and can lead on to more serious alcohol dependency issues.

Make sure your bed is made and comfortable with dim lighting in the bedroom. Tidy your bedroom too. Sleeping in chaos can keep you awake at night.

Make your bedroom primarily a place for sleeping. It is not a good idea to use your bed for watching TV, doing work, etc. Help your body recognize that this is a place for rest or intimacy.

I shall be clean

Hide your clock. A big, illuminated digital clock may cause you to focus on the time and make you feel stressed and anxious. Place your clock so you can't see the time when you are in bed.

Check the temperature. Try to keep a constant temperature so you are neither too hot nor too cold and make sure there are no draughts.

Give yourself some winding down time before going to bed. Try the relaxation exercise from chapter seven. Read or listen to music. Try listening to recorded relaxation or guided imagery programs.

Have a warm bath with some Lavender oil in.

Make yourself a warm milky drink. Although be aware that drinking too much fluid before bed can cause you to get up to urinate.

Put your thoughts and feelings to bed soon. Nothing can be resolved in the middle of the night. If you need to write down your worries and possible solutions before you go to bed. A journal or "to do" list may be very helpful in letting you put away these concerns until the next day when you are fresh.

Exercise Fourteen

If you are seriously considering stopping.

Let's put together a plan to support that decision using tools and strategies learned in this book and any that you have in your own internal toolbox.

These may be things that have worked for you in the past:

I shall be clean

STOP DATE:

(Put down a date that you plan to stop)

THINGS THAT MAY CAUSE A RELAPSE	STRATEGIES I HAVE FOR THOSE SITUATIONS
Places I may go	
Fred's house	Stay away for the time being. Then ask him not to use when I visit as I am trying to stop.

Things I may do	
Listen to music	Heavy music is my trigger so listen to more calming music

Things I might see	
Spoons	Bin all my paraphernalia and anything that reminds me of drugs

I shall be clean

Things I might feel	
Angry	Read the anger management pages in this book and use these skills to manage my anger

Things I might smell, taste or hear	
Cannabis	Avoid places where I might smell this for the time being

Thoughts I may have	
"I'm worthless"	Use my imagery to challenge this thought before believing it to be true

I shall be clean

Things may happen to me	
My girlfriend falls out with me	Manage my emotions with a distraction technique

Ways in which I might refuse drugs:
"No thanks I have a busy day tomorrow and need to wake up refreshed"

And last but not least here is a story for you to read:

THE CARPENTER

An elderly carpenter was feeling ready to retire. He told his employer of his plans to leave the house building business and live a more leisurely life with his wife and family.

His employer was sorry to see such a good worker go, and asked him if he could build just one more house as a personal favour. The carpenter said "Yes", but in time it was easy to see that

I shall be clean

his heart was not in his work. His workmanship was shoddy and he used inferior materials.

It was an unfortunate way to end such a dedicated career.

When the carpenter had finished his work, his employer came to inspect the house.

He handed the front door keys to the carpenter "This is your house" he said "My gift to you for your loyal work". The carpenter was shocked! What a shame! If he had only known that he was building his own house, he would have done it all so differently!

(So it is with all of us. We build our lives, a day at a time, often putting less than our best into the building. Then with a shock we have to live in the house we have 'built'.

If we could do it again, we would do it differently. But we cannot go back, however we can move forward.)

You are the carpenter of your life. Life is a 'do it yourself project'

Your attitudes and the choices you make today, build the 'house' you live in tomorrow.

BUILD WISELY!

The next chapter is for your parents, friends and family to read, guidance on how to support you in your recovery. You may not like some of the guidance but sometimes it is about 'tough love' and often it is that, that facilitates change.

I have lost count of the amount of clients that changed their drug use when parents stopped rescuing them, buying their drugs for them, bailing them out of all sorts of bother.

You are an adult now and must take responsibility for your own behaviour which is not healthy for you. This guidance supports your growth into a health functioning grown up.

I shall be clean

May I take this opportunity to wish you all the best in your recovery.

I believe you can do it, now you just have to believe in yourself too.

I shall be clean

CHAPTER TWELVE
Parents Carers family and friends of drug users

I have added this chapter in my book as I am aware that family and friends may need some understanding on their loved ones substance misuse.

Many of the calls that are taken at substance misuse services are from anxious family members about their loved ones and their concerns that they are taking drugs. There expectation often is that we can tell from the descriptions that they give us over the phone whether their child/husband etc is using drugs.

The truth is we cannot always tell just as family members cannot always tell. Unless there is evident paraphernalia around we cannot always tell by their behaviour. People behave in many different ways for many different reasons.

Some of the symptoms of adolescence for example can mirror some of the symptoms of drug use. Some of the symptoms of mental health problems can mirror the symptoms of substance misuse.

The best thing you can do as a parent/partner or family member or friend is to communicate in a non judgemental way, listen to what your loved one says to you, and as difficult as it is to try not to act on your emotions if your loved one disclosed that s/he is using drugs.

Try to stay calm. To react in a negative way will just send your loved one underground and then you will not be in a position to support him/her in getting into treatment.

I shall be clean

Although this is guidance for parents. It can be used for any family member that is supporting a drug user:

THE PARENT AS AN ENABLER

The following information is to help you to understand:

> **The difference between enabling and helping**
>
> **What behaviours constitutes enabling**
>
> **Your own enabling behaviours and help to facilitate change in those behaviours**

HELPING is doing something for someone that he not capable of doing himself

ENABLING is doing for someone what he could do for himself

ENABLING CREATES AN ATMOSPHERE IN WHICH OUR ADULT CHILDREN CAN COMFORTABLY CONTINUE THEIR UNACCEPTABLE BEHAVIOUR

ENABLING IS:

> When we continue to allow unacceptable behaviour,
>
> When we are setting up a pattern with our children that will be hard to change
>
> When we've been repeating the same patterns for years.

I shall be clean

WHY DO WE ENABLE:

> When we confuse 'helping' with 'enabling'
> When we fear for our safety
> When we irrationally fear for their safety
> When we are worried about consequences
> When we feel guilty about things we did or didn't do when they were younger
> When it is all we know how to do (habit)
> It feels easier than change
> Not knowing how to stop

THE CONSEQUENCES OF ENABLING:

> When we continue this behaviour our adult children will continue to deny that they have any problems, since most of them are being 'solved' by the people around them.
>
> It will be hard for our adult children to develop tools for coping with their lot in life.
>
> Our adult children will learn to expect us to deal with all their problems.
>
> We will consistently be worn out and unable to move forward with our own lives.
>
> When we enable it is all about our child and not about us and our needs and goals

I shall be clean

ONLY WHEN THEY ARE FORCED TO FACE THE CONSEQUENCES OF THEIR OWN ACTIONS AND CHOICES, WILL IT FINALLY BEGIN TO SINK IN HOW DEEP THEIR OWN PATTERNS OF DEPENDENCE AND AVOIDANCE HAVE BECOME.

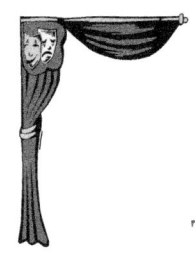

TAKE THE SPOTLIGHT OFF YOUR CHILD!!!

IN THE DRAMA OF YOUR CHILDS LIFE, YOU'VE NOT ONLY BEEN THE DIRECTOR BUT THE PRODUCER, STAGEMANAGER DRESSER, CATERER,.FINANCER, SCRIPT WRITER., EDITOR ETC.

THIS SHOW IS NOW OVER!
A NEW PRODUCTION IS NOW NEEDED!
YOU ARE THE STAR NOW!

I shall be clean

CHANGE IS HARD:

If you have been an enabling parent, it will be difficult to change. However our focus is on helping the parent to change their own behaviours and responses, not those of the adult child.

Change is needed to stop the pain, stop the excuses and come to a resolution.

We need to stop trying to change their behaviour by making choices/excuses for them and by shielding them from the painful consequences of their actions or inaction.

We cannot change others we can only change ourselves, but by changing ourselves it will inadvertently change others.

You can't change someone else, but you can change your response to them. This then invites a different response from them; they may respond this way and change.

Be warned that our children did not get this way overnight, so they won't change overnight – However as we start to change our behaviours, change will happen more quickly when we are not enabling.

We need to set boundaries!

I shall be clean

SIX STEPS TO SANITY

S = Stop your own negative behaviour (especially the flow of money)

A = Assemble support

N = Nip excuses in the bud

I = Implement rules and boundaries

T = Trust your instincts

Y = Yield (Learn to let go of what you cannot change)

SETTING AND KEEPING BOUNDARIES:

A boundary is a limit on what is reasonable

They help to clarify what are acceptable and unacceptable behaviours from others

Effective boundaries are the foundation of all healthy relationships; they help to develop trust, stability and respect

Families of substance users can set boundaries to limit the behaviour of the user to what is considered reasonable

Setting boundaries asserts the needs or rights of families so that they feel secure and respected

KEY AREAS TO LOOK AT WHEN SETTING BOUNDARIES:

I shall be clean

YOUR TIME: Time is an important personal asset. Does your child drop by unexpectedly? Do they make unreasonable demands on your time? Do they expect you to change your plans?

YOUR EMOTIONS: Your emotions are where your love and caring comes from. They should be well protected. Does your child say or do hurtful things (often unintentional)? Been thoughtless? Does he hook into your emotions and manipulate this?

YOUR ENERGY: Your energy comes from your inner peace, your activities, your personal time etc. Does your child invade your privacy, make unreasonable demands? This means that you are unable to function effectively.

YOUR SAFETY: Do you feel threatened? Do you feel at risk?

YOUR HOME AND PROPERTY: Does your child make threats against your possessions? Do they steal from you? Do they treat your house like a hotel?

We have been sending mixed messages for years about what is acceptable and what isn't, what we'll tolerate and what we won't.

We have perfected the boy-who-cried-wolf syndrome by not establishing and sticking with firm boundaries and consequences.

DEFINING BOUNDARIES:

We need to have a clearly defined action plan before confronting our children

I shall be clean

> We need to establish consequences and stick with them
>
> We need to present a unified front if in a relationship
>
> We must not get involved in a debate or discussion
>
> We need to encourage our adult children to figure things out for themselves
>
> We need to ask ourselves "Who am I outside of this issue/child?
>
> We must be willing to shift the focus off the life of our adult child, and onto our own.

We must also value ourselves and take care of us. We are worth this so make a commitment to 'taking care of YOU!

KEEP CALM AND PRACTICE SELF-CARE

I shall be clean

**Suggestions for breaking the enabling cycle:
A commitment contract to yourself**

1. I shall take care of my own spiritual, mental, physical, emotional and financial health
2. I shall remember to express love and attention to my partner and other family member and friends in addition to my troubled adult child
3. I shall not accept excuses
4. I shall understand that a clear definition of right and wrong is imperative
5. I shall make fact based judgements without excuse or feeling guilty
6. I shall uphold standards of behaviour that protect my morals, values and integrity
7. I shall give my adult child unconditional love and support without meddling and without money
8. I shall celebrate life and love as often as possible even in times of trouble
9. I shall define my goals as they relate to my life, not to the life of my adult child
10. I shall make my decisions based on long term goals, not short term remedies; and act accordingly

Signed..

Date:..

I shall be clean

TAKING ACTION:

> The first commitment is to stop this enabling pattern
>
> Better to do it in "one fell swoop" rather than dragging it out
>
> Dragging it out sends mixed messages to our adult children and it is hard on us as carers to volley back and forth between enabling behaviour and clear boundaries
>
> Therefore we need a plan!

Developing an action plan:

> It is okay to state your wish for their future, but that this future is ultimately their choice
>
> Be clear about changes you are making
>
> Don't point fingers, try not to say "you" too much.
>
> Tell your adult child that you've made a U-Turn, you're changing and there is no going back
>
> It's okay to tell them that you have been enabling (rescuing)
>
> If you want them to move out tell them so and give them a firm move out date as well as a firm consequence
>
> Define consequences for every item on your list, you might want to consider issues around rent, laundry, curfew, zero tolerance for drugs/alcohol, food, debt, getting up in the

I shall be clean

morning etc
Tell them what you are willing to do to support them.

Remain consistent, love them and follow up on all consequences

Tell them what you will not do i.e. state that you will not give them money, you will not argue or negotiate, you will not make excuses, you will not pay debts/fines, you will not accept blame.

Develop a list of resources for your adult child e.g.: details of drug/alcohol treatment agencies, useful numbers to call, self help groups, books, debt counsellors etc.

Develop a transition care package – be careful about this part as we don't want to give them too much or do things on their behalf.

However there may be some instances where some additional help might make this transition easier e.g.: If you ask them to move out, you may want to give them supermarket coupons, or a pre-pay phone card, or some household items etc. You should also give them important documents like birth certificates, medical history etc.

Planning:

We are going to develop a written plan that clearly indicates your goals. It will help you to review where you are and where you want to go.

This plan will be spoken with love and not in heated anger or frustration – it will help you to be objective

You are bringing this plan to the judgement table, not the

I shall be clean

negotiating table

You are the adult and this is your home, your money, your livelihood and your future and the time has come for you to define acceptable boundaries and to commit to them.

So, first of all write down the issues that are not acceptable to you:

1.
2.
3.
4.
5.

Now what we need to do is set some acceptable boundaries:

1.
2.
3.
4.
5.

Presenting your action plan:

1. Find the right time to have the discussion

2. Present it with a concern for their long term wellbeing but try not to get overly emotional

3. Type it up if possible – make it like a formal business contract and if you can, get them to sign it

4. Don't present it as changes that they need to make, don't

I shall be clean

say "you need to do this". As the parent making the behaviour changes you need to inform your adult child that YOU have had a problem and therefore YOU are changing the way that you respond and behave. They can choose to change their behaviour – or not

5. Remember, you can't MAKE them tidy their room, but you can stop paying their mobile phone bill for example

6. Don't use the word "but" – contracts don't have escape clauses

7. Consider the consequences – they will find it difficult, it might be hard for you to watch them hurt. However this is part of the process and they have to get desperate enough to make changes.

8. Ask someone for support if you need it.

Don't be surprised if it is met with resistance – this is the sign that you are doing the right thing.

If you enable or rescue your child you are disempowering them from making the right decisions for him/her. Permanent change only happens when people make the decision themselves.

I hope that this has been helpful.

I shall be clean

Final Words

Well this is the end of my self help book for substance misuse.

Most families in society today will have at least one member of their family or extended family either dependent on drugs or have experimented with drugs. If you are a family that haven't then you are lucky.

For the last ten years the government has focused on 'harm reduction', in terms of substance misuse treatment. This was extremely important for several reasons, to minimise drug related deaths, to stop the spread of blood borne viruses and to reduce crime.

The focus now is on recovery, and although for people working within substance misuse services, recovery has always been on the agenda, that is in my eyes a good move.

Part of that recovery plan though needs to be 'the removal' of these illegal pharmacies on the street. Unfortunately these groups will always target our young people, people that are vulnerable and susceptible to experimenting with something that is not good for them, and people will always sell what is seen as profitable, what makes them money.

Financial greed that does not consider the impact that the products they are selling are harming others and the impact that it has on society. It harms their customers, their customers families and friends and society. The knock on effect their products have on us is indefensible. Their consciences are in the gutter.

In my experience raids on 'dealers' were done on a regular

I shall be clean

basis by police, but just like the employment market today, when ten people 'lose their jobs' there is another twenty people waiting to take their place.

I would like to share with you an interesting conversation with a client who I was working with, a heavy stimulant user who had been drug free for a month:

> "My dealer knocked on the door yesterday Linda",
> "Did he?"
> "Yes, he's not very happy that I'm not using anymore, in fact he was quite angry"
> "Oh"
> "He says he can't go on holiday now that I have stopped using"

It appears that dealers don't get holiday pay, like the rest of us, what a shame!

This appears to be what they are spending your money on. Whilst you are struggling to eat, have a social life, get out of this rut, they are spending YOUR money on holidays, cars, food, designer clothes and a roof over their head. Whilst some addicts are sofa surfing.

Think about what you can buy and achieve once you stop handing over your money to these unscrupulous people.

I sincerely hope that this book has helped you to work towards recovery or at the very least think about change.

I shall be clean

I would like to make one final dedication:

**To my cousin who died in 2010 from a drug and alcohol related death.
Rest in peace.**

Website: www.linda-mather.co.uk
E-Mail: mather_linda@sky.com

I shall be clean

Printed in Great Britain
by Amazon